Forms of Farewell

Desire prolongs its adventure to create
Forms of farewell . . .

—"An Ordinary Evening in New Haven"

For My Parents
and Mary

Forms of Farewell

The Late Poetry of Wallace Stevens

Charles Berger

THE UNIVERSITY OF WISCONSIN PRESS

Published 1985

The University of Wisconsin Press
114 North Murray Street
Madison, Wisconsin 53715

The University of Wisconsin Press, Ltd.
1 Gower Street
London WC1E 6HA, England

First printing

Printed in the United States of America

For LC CIP information see the colophon

ISBN 0-299-09920-2

Contents

Preface

This book offers a reading of the major poems, long and short, of Wallace Stevens' last decade and provides a shape, or a plot, to the final movement of his career. So while I have tried always to be equal to the verbal subtlety of his poetry, I have also looked for the guiding concerns or obsessions that make the phrase "late poetry," in Stevens' case at least, so much more than a chronological description. My argument begins by trying to understand the way in which "Esthétique du Mal" and "The Auroras of Autumn" can be considered war poems: how do they use poetry to defend against the reality of total war, the apocalyptic threat to civilization itself? One can argue that Stevens' late poetry begins in an atmosphere of premature closure, as Stevens fears that the war will bring on a sudden end to civilized life. When these fears subside, we get poems that I have called counterapocalyptic, such as "Credences of Summer" and "An Ordinary Evening in New Haven," poems which begin to see the world as *saved*. The book's final two chapters are given to "The Owl in the Sarcophagus" and the last poems, those "forms of farewell" in which Stevens meditates on and creates his own legacy.

I can trace the origin of my preoccupation with

these issues to two "incidents" in my reading of Stevens. One came when I first suspected that the apocalyptic drama of "The Auroras of Autumn" might be connected to the war, and that the auroras themselves might be seen as a figuration of the atomic bomb. After this, I could no longer remain satisfied with thinking of "Auroras" only in terms of the theater of the mind. The shadow of a new sphere of reference had passed over the poem. My second personal source could be located in a single line from the very late poem "The Planet on the Table," where Stevens/Ariel, speaking of his poems, says: "It was not important that they survive." While I knew that I could not accept this statement at face value, I began to ask myself: what *was* Stevens' attitude toward literary survival? With this thought in mind, I saw how many of the late lyrics pondered this issue in mysterious and powerful ways. This helped me in turn to gather a sense of cohesiveness about these poems, whose overall "direction" had always proved opaque to me. I realized that Stevens wrote his own elegy over and over again, as he attempted to place himself in the afterlife of literary history.

Taken out of context, these "originating" moments sound starkly thematic, as if I were proposing a key to the understanding of late Stevens. My intention, though, is not to make Stevens easier to read by reducing the ambiguities inherent in his work. I would rather call attention to the converging forces of history and literary history that can make him so difficult. For the deepening inwardness of Stevens' poetry has nothing to do with hermeticism. His refusal to write accessible, public poetry does not mean that he ignored the pressures that drove other poets to do so. Indeed, the rigors of Stevens' late style register such pressures at every turn. Not to see this is to narrow the scope of his work and to underestimate the nature of his poetic ambition. War is the great antagonist of the imagination precisely because it can engage the imagination so seductively. But survival—for the poet and his civilization, the poet *in* his civilization—is the higher strain to which Stevens testifies throughout his later poetry.

A word about the boundaries of this study, or at least the near boundary. I begin with "Esthétique du Mal" rather than "Notes toward a Supreme Fiction" because the former betrays the pressure of apocalyptic thinking to a much greater extent. "Notes" is a poem of summation, an encyclopedic poem which gathers together all that the poet knows in the face of a possible ending, but the poem seems to disguise the nature of its effort. To a greater degee than "Esthétique" or "Auroras" or "An Ordinary Evening in New Haven," it is a poem of masks, guises, personae.

As I worked through the poems covered in this book, I came to recognize the importance of Yeats for Stevens. Yeats closing out his poetic career, writing his *Last Poems*, must have struck Stevens as exemplary, especially his way of viewing external violence within the context of his own death. How does the poet provide for his survival when the very civilization supposed to mediate his fame is itself on the point of destruction? In certain moments, to be sure, Yeats greeted such violence with approval, regarding his own future as more akin to the order that would presumably follow such upheaval. At other moments, he sought to lodge his poetic image in a memorial sufficiently "natural" to withstand all assaults. The kinds of metaphors for the poet's legacy developed by Yeats would have both fascinated and antagonized Stevens. But even beyond the particulars of Yeats's vision, the spectacle of such a poet making or fashioning his end, especially after a long career, would have commanded Stevens' full attention. So I find Yeats crucial to my arguments at a number of points, in this sense revising Harold Bloom's emphasis in *The Poems of Our Climate* on Whitman and Emerson—and indeed the *precursor* generally—as the predominant source of influence. Bloom's theory compels us to think in terms of origins, as if all examples of influence were best seen as repetitions, however varied, of the initial and massive contact between new poet and precursor which he has called the "scene of instruction." Much more needs to be said on this subject, but I hope that the way in which I bring Yeats into my account of Stevens will reveal the kind of dialogue between contemporaries which is not based on priority and hence might display clearer conceptual differences. And yet one might always respond that Stevens was quarreling with Yeats for the right to represent the true romantic tradition.

Speaking of influences, my work has been sustained by creative agreements and disagreements with the two major books on Stevens, Helen Vendler's *On Extended Wings*[1] and Harold Bloom's *The Poems of Our Climate.*[2] As a quick look at my endnotes and a close reading of my prose will prove, these books have been much more than casual reference points. Three other works come specifically to mind when I think of what has been most helpful to me. Frank Kermode's *The Sense of an Ending*[3] has been the key text against which to measure assertions about the nature of Stevens' peculiar apocalyptic vision. Kermode's discussion of the traditional rhetoric of apocalypse, combined with his skeptical distrust of facile uses of the term, has stayed with me. Lawrence Lipking's *The Life of the Poet*[4] provided many pages of elegant and powerful aperçus on the characteristic metaphors for literary survival. Lipking does not study Stevens' final poems, but much of what he says about Rilke and Mallarmé, for example, would be more than applicable to Stevens. Finally, an essay by Richard Poirier in the first volume of *Raritan*, entitled "Writing Off the Self,"[5] addressed the very issues I wanted to raise in my reading of Stevens, although with different emphasis. For Poirier would question the assumption that poets always want to survive, want to attain the immortality of literary fame. He argues for the presence of a counterimpulse, one that wishes to "eradicate the human self." Taking issue with Bloom, Poirier writes:

> As I read Stevens' poetry, much of it does not finally show the anxieties about the human presence or the necessity for assertions of the human will that are central in Harold Bloom's account of it. . . . Criticism, with its emphasis on structures that must develop rather than recede, apparently finds it nearly impossible to recognize the quite casual way in which literature calls us sometimes to witness the disappearance of the human.[6]

Sentences such as these helped me to find the center of my argument, for I could not quite believe that Stevens was ever casual about the disappearance of the human. And yet every reader of Stevens knows exactly the kind of reductive or minimalist movement to which Poirier refers. And though Poirier goes on to warn against finding an overly easy act of restitution in Stevens, whereby the human returns, I think that precisely such a process does occur throughout Stevens' late poetry, though it is anything but easy. For this return merges with the question of poetic afterlife, so that the poet's ability to imagine his form of survival both depends upon and guarantees our own, through the strenuous and loving process of attentiveness we call reading.

Acknowledgments

It is a great pleasure to thank friends and colleagues who have shared their wisdom and humor with me. In their company, the lost art of conversation is always rediscovered. In particular, let me mention: Harold Bloom, Leslie Brisman, Richard Brodhead, Robert Caserio, Michael Cooke, Paul Fry, William Galperin, Joseph Gordon, Dori Hale, Geoffrey Hartman, John Hollander, Nicholas Howe, Nancy Huddleston Packer, Lelia Ruckenstein, and Samuel Schulman. I would also like to express my gratitude to the students in the seminars on Stevens that I taught at Yale. Much of this book started there. Yale University has been generous in its support: a Morse Fellowship helped me write this book, and a grant from the Griswold Fund helped in the preparation of the manuscript. Finally, I am grateful to the libraries of the University of California at Berkeley and Washington University for making their resources available to me.

Acknowledgment is made to Alfred A. Knopf, Inc. and to Faber and Faber Ltd. for permission to quote from the following copyrighted works of Wallace Stevens: *The Collected Poems of Wallace Stevens*; *Souvenirs and Prophecies*: *The Young Wallace*

Stevens, by Holly Stevens; *Letters of Wallace Stevens*, edited by Holly Stevens; *The Necessary Angel*; and *Opus Posthumous*, edited by Samuel French Morse.

Permission to quote from the writings of W. B. Yeats has been granted by The Macmillan Publishing Company, Inc. and by Michael B. Yeats and Macmillan London Ltd. The following works are from *The Poems of W. B. Yeats*, edited by Richard J. Finneran, The Macmillan Publishing Company, Inc.: "Lapis Lazuli," copyright 1940, Georgie Yeats, renewed 1968 by Bertha Yeats, Michael B. Yeats, and Anne Yeats; "In Memory of Eva Gore-Booth and Con Markiewicz" and "Byzantium," copyright 1933 The Macmillan Publishing Company, Inc., renewed 1961 by Bertha Georgie Yeats; "A Prayer for My Daughter," copyright 1924 The Macmillan Publishing Company, Inc., renewed 1952 by Bertha Georgie Yeats; "He Hears the Cry of the Sedge," copyright 1983 The Macmillan Publishing Company, Inc.

Permission to quote from "Fragment" in *The Double Dream of Spring* has been granted by Georges Borchardt, Inc. and John Ashbery, copyright 1970 by John Ashbery.

Forms of Farewell

I

"Esthétique du Mal": Under the Volcano

Stevens' first poem written under the volcano—"A Postcard from the Volcano" (1936)—is a prophetic elegy for a lost civilization or culture:

Children picking up our bones
Will never know that these were once
As quick as foxes on the hill;

And that in autumn, when the grapes
Made sharp air sharper by their smell
These had a being, breathing frost;

And least will guess that with our bones
We left much more, left what still is
The look of things, left what we felt

At what we saw. The spring clouds blow
Above the shuttered mansion-house
Beyond our gate and the windy sky

Cries out a literate despair.
We knew for long the mansion's look
And what we said of it became

A part of what it is . . . Children,

Still weaving budded aureoles,
Will speak our speech and never know,

Will say of the mansion that it seems
As if he that lived there left behind
A spirit storming in blank walls,

A dirty house in a gutted world,
A tatter of shadows peaked to white,
Smeared with the gold of the opulent sun.[1]

It is possible, of course, to view this situation as simply a drastic way of describing the reading process: "Children picking up our bones" may as well be picking up our books, for all that they will come to know of the author's true life. Yet I think the poem cries out for a wider frame of reference, although the scope of destruction that it portends remains necessarily vague. "The shuttered mansion-house" can be made as large or as small as we like: the abode of one poet or of a whole people. We need only multiply the particulars of loss, so acutely rendered by Stevens. Similarly, we are free to adjust the poem's implicit time line, the interval between the lost inhabitants of the mansion and the children who came after them, the temporal gap widening in accord with the scale of devastation. And yet perhaps only the sense of an interval is important, destruction bringing on a new chronology in its wake. All these issues come to center upon the enigmatic "children" and the questions they raise of relation and inheritance. Whatever satisfaction might be taken in their survival is dashed by their ignorance of us, of their origins. On the one hand, they continue to speak "our speech" (seen here as a natural language, a language of the earth), yet they are incapable of deciphering the "blank walls" of our artifacts. Only the legacy of anonymous speech survives that part of us which has merged with, but also changed, "what we saw." Catastrophe has leveled the more individuating monuments, whether poems or buildings. This postcard alone has survived.

But the true predecessor poem to "Esthétique du Mal" is "Extracts from Addresses to the Academy of Fine Ideas" (1940), a poem in which the potential scale of violence in the new war ("total war," in Stevens' words) begins to weigh on the poet. A more diffuse poem than "Esthétique," and lacking a central image such as the volcano, "Extracts" nevertheless offers startling passages on the dangerous esthetics of catastrophe and the likely end of total war. The poem's second section addresses the phenomenon, all too common among Stevens' contemporaries, of esthetic complicity in the crimes of the age:

> Let the Secretary for Porcelain observe
> That evil made magic, as in catastrophe,
> If neatly glazed, becomes the same as the fruit
> Of an emperor, the egg-plant of a prince.
> The good is evil's last invention. Thus
> The maker of catastrophe invents the eye
> And through the eye equates ten thousand deaths
> With a single well-tempered apricot, or, say,
> An egg-plant of good air.

The eye that wore "le monocle" is certainly as fine an appraiser of glazed *objets* as one would want, but that Stevens distances himself from this sort of esthetic distancing is made abundantly clear by the end of "Extracts." He does this first of all by establishing our *bond* to the earth as a "belief in one's element." To show how powerful and necessary a belief this is, Stevens imagines a mental traveler capable of abandoning earth for "The moon, / Or anywhere beyond." Upon his return, such a journeyer would realize the extent to which the earth is our "subtle centre." Stevens wants us to carry the realization of our "ecstatic identity" with earth over into the final section of "Extracts," where he rises to consider the consequences of war's violations:

> We live in a camp . . . Stanzas of final peace
> Lie in the heart's residuum . . . Amen.
> But would it be amen, in choirs, if once
> In total war we died and after death
> Returned, unable to die again, fated
> To endure thereafter every mortal wound,
> Beyond a second death, as evil's end?
>
> It is only that we are able to die, to escape
> The wounds. Yet to lie buried in evil earth,
> If evil never ends, is to return
> To evil after death, unable to die
> Again and fated to endure beyond
> Any mortal end. The chants of final peace
> Lie in the heart's residuum.
>
> How can
> We chant if we live in evil and afterward
> Lie harshly buried there?
>
> If earth dissolves
> Its evil after death, it dissolves it while
> We live. Thence come the final chants, the chants
> Of the brooder seeking the acutest end
> Of speech: to pierce the heart's residuum
> And there to find music for a single line,
> Equal to memory, one line in which
> The vital music formulates the words.
>
> Behold the men in helmets borne on steel,
> Discolored, how they are going to defeat.

We have turned the planet into an armed camp. Earth's "subtle centre," within us, has hardened into a residue; the poet's job is to pierce the deep heart's core and release the potential for peace. Stevens expands the notion of total war to include the astonishing idea that death, or at least the peacefulness of death, can itself be slain, since we have so befouled our burial ground. Bridging the gap between the question "How can / We chant," and the possible answer "If earth dissolves / Its evils," would be the poem's major leap of faith, bringing together the health of the world and our own songs. At stake is no less than whether or not "We live": Stevens isolates the words at the beginning of the line here, but they become the final two words of "Esthétique du Mal," whose final section brings the chant into being.

The best characterization of the figure Stevens presents at the opening of "Esthétique du Mal" can be found in a poem written two years later, "Mountains Covered with Cats":

> Regard the invalid personality
> Instead, outcast, without the will to power
> And impotent, like the imagination seeking
> To propagate the imagination or like
> War's miracle begetting that of peace.

Stevens' invalid—for "Mal" has more to do with malady than evil—has certainly lost the will to power. He manages to write only letters, read no more than paragraphs, and he must advert himself from Vesuvius in order to accomplish even this. Once Stevens drops any direct link to this opening persona, the poem can begin to consider figures of resolute, if sometimes perverse, will—those who are able to center their obsessions. True strength breaks out only at the poem's close.

It is good to remember, as we read the opening sections of "Esthétique," that Naples was a war zone in 1944. (Those "letters home" are a parody of the war correspondent's cables.) The effort to render contemporary violence always turned Stevens more than usually oblique, and here he fashions a pallid alter ego who can read present calamity only by its ancient signs. The theory of the sublime, by teaching us how to describe Vesuvius, has in a sense contained it:

> He could describe
> The terror of the sound because the sound
> Was ancient. He tried to remember the phrases: pain
> Audible at noon, pain torturing itself,
> Pain killing pain on the very point of pain.

So the theory goes. Stevens skews it by displaying a case where figurative language, hypostatized into the Book, is powerless to correct catastrophe: his ailing poet has developed a kind of counterstutter, one which blocks him from pronouncing any word other than the painful one. He can no longer substitute the saving if somber figurations of the sublime for the literal torment afflicting him. The book he either reads or composes tries to accommodate itself to the destructive principle by assuming a pose of stoic indifference toward both past and imminent apocalypse. But Emerson's injunction in his essay "Fate," to "embrace the force that crushes you,"[2] seems to crush this poet prematurely; the enjambment at the beginning of canto II—"he lay / On his balcony at night"—shows him neatly suspended between life and death. The messages sent by sleep, though at variance with the sublime, also provide little comfort. Their power is seen as "the intelligence of despair," which is rejected on esthetic grounds as being "Too dark, too far, too much the accents of / Afflicted sleep."

This portrait of refined impotence is caricature of the subtlest kind. I hesitate to call it self-caricature, even though it is clear that Stevens is once again using the third-person pronoun as a way of lancing (or at least recognizing) dangerous tendencies in himself. As in "Landscape with Boat" or "Anglais Mort à Florence," the elegiac tone serves both to distance and dissect—the elegy becomes a postmortem, a display of Stevens' "'scholarly' interest in his own pain," as Helen Vendler puts it.[3] In this case, pain comes from a keen sense of powerlessness in the face of catastrophe. Salves for that pain are proposed throughout the poem, but not until its final chant do we come upon one that seems trustworthy, a "cure of ourselves, that is equal to a cure of the ground." But Stevens is deeply seductive when using inspired rhetoric to purvey false cures. The "kind of elegy" which the exiled poet finds upon turning to the moon, emblem of loneliness, almost survives the most skeptical reading. The passage never falters in its eloquence, even as it presents a kind of submissiveness which becomes elegiac:

> The moon rose up as if it had escaped
> His meditation. It evaded his mind.
> It was part of a supremacy always
> Above him. The moon was always free from him,
> As night was free from him. The shadow touched
> Or merely seemed to touch him as he spoke
> A kind of elegy he found in space:

> It is pain that is indifferent to the sky
> In spite of the yellow of the acacias, the scent
> Of them in the air still hanging heavily
> In the hoary-hanging night. It does not regard
> This freedom, this supremacy, and in
> Its own hallucination never sees
> How that which rejects it saves it in the end.

The moon is posited as a friend to man here, saving him from his own injurious phantoms. The moon is firmly and objectively other, even if somewhat shadowy; by ignoring us it actually comes to relieve us of our obsessions. Pain, however, remains "indifferent" to this offer of comfort, and that grudging word inclines us to the view that to embrace "This freedom, this supremacy" is right. Yet whose freedom is this? we might ask. And what is given up by accepting such supremacy? Since the final seven lines of canto II are called "a kind of elegy," there is the further question of who or what has died. To see what is most troubling about this passage, all the reader need do is juxtapose it with the final lines of the poem, where the emphasis falls heavily on the infinitive "to make," and where the very last words, "we live," banish both the elegiac and the submissive. The afflicted poet of the opening cantos, however legitimate the sources of his pain—and Stevens must often have felt a sense of impotence in time of war—fails the test of strength. The elegy records his capitulation to a version of fate, and he disappears from the poem.

"Esthétique du Mal" is best read as a procession of attitudes or postures assumed under the volcano. The poem certainly features a multiplicity of perspectives, even if the claim to "many *selves*" which

Stevens makes at the end seems too full-bodied. Canto III introduces a new and short-lived persona: "His firm stanzas hang like hives in hell." Ghosts of the Neapolitan setting perhaps still flutter here, since southern Italy is the site of the entrance to the underworld in Virgil. Then there is the peculiar resonance for Stevens of the verb "hang"; as with Eliot's fear of the Hanged Man, Stevens sees dangling shapes as ominous end signs. "We hang like warty squashes," says the uncle in "Le Monocle," foreseeing the grotesque conclusion of his love; "Shall we be found hanging in the trees next spring?" is the most fateful question in "Auroras"; in "The Course of a Particular" the end is near when we can say merely that "Today the leaves cry, hanging on branches swept by wind."[4]

These infernal "hives" mock the analogy between poetry and nature, but they might also signal the poet's prophetic mission, as the infernal bough does in Virgil. Voice deepens momentarily with the declaration, in rhyming tercet, that the triple realms of earth, heaven, and hell are now united:

> His firm stanzas hang like hives in hell
> Or what hell was, since now both heaven and hell
> Are one, and here, o terra infidel.

Normally, Stevens celebrates the grounding of religious categories in an earthly here and now. But this bitter apostrophe to earth suggests that nature can indeed betray the heart that loves her. More is involved than the volcano's power to eradicate us and know none of our pain, since the next series of accusations is aimed at "an over-human god" who is faulted precisely for taking too much of our pain upon him. Stevens is not one to cast either nature or god in the role of scapegoat, and at this point in the poem one begins to see why its author once defined the word "Esthétique" in his title as "the equivalent of aperçus."[5] One would not claim a higher status for the proposal that "The fault lies with an over-human god," a Nietzscheanism designed to turn us from amelioration toward "our fate." A truer voice takes over, as it so often does in Stevens, after the dissolving break of an ellipsis:

> A too, too human god, self-pity's kin
> And uncourageous genesis . . . It seems
> As if the health of the world might be enough.
>
> It seems as if the honey of common summer
> might be enough. . . .

Hell has been transformed to health and hives into honey. Such health will be explored at the end of this poem, and in the closing canto of "The Auroras of Autumn," while common summer receives its day in "Credences of Summer."

By the end of canto III, both human and inhuman deities (or anodynes) have been banished from the poem, leaving us only with a qualified sense of emancipation—"as if we were sure to find our way"— and eagerness to hear some wisdom on the broached question of the relationship between inner pain and catastrophic events. It comes as no surprise when Stevens announces that it is "that evil, that evil in the self," which is the source of our woe:

> The genius of misfortune
> Is not a sentimentalist. He is
> That evil, that evil in the self, from which
> In desperate hallow, rugged gesture, fault
> Falls out on everything: the genius of
> The mind, which is our being, wrong and wrong,

> The genius of the body, which is our world,
> Spent in the false engagements of the mind.

"Fault / Falls": the enjambment and the wordplay are Miltonic, but the notion of the Fall as an event located solely in our consciousness is closer to Blake and Shelley. "Engagements of the mind," with the military sense foregrounded, is pure Stevens, hearkening back to the doctrine of the mind's destructiveness codified in "Man and Bottle." The passage points, overtly enough, to a wasteful dualism as the source of war and pain, but it is really the obsessive or compulsive character of mental life, as much as its misguidedness, which Stevens singles out for villainy.

With this in mind, the esthetic parables concerning B. (almost certainly Brahms, Stevens' favorite composer, the "dark familiar" of "Anglais Mort à Florence") and a more mysterious "Spaniard of the Rose"—can it really be the horticulturist Pedro Dot?[6]—take a more sinister interpretation. B. is pictured as a hedgehog, rather than a fox, to use Isaiah Berlin's famous distinction, an artist who draws strength from holding hard to the single truths which obsess him:

> When B. sat down at the piano and made
> A transparence in which we heard music, made music,
> In which we heard transparent sounds, did he play
> All sorts of notes? Or did he play only one
> In an ecstasy of its associates . . .

The poetic line enacts this apparent movement toward reductiveness, as "all" is narrowed down to "one"; but we hardly need "ecstasy of its associates" to assure us that Stevens looks favorably upon such rich austerity. "The Well Dressed Man with a Beard" waxed ecstatic on the score of "One only, one thing that was firm." Finding the true note is akin to discovering one's fate. Thoughout this section of "Esthétique," Stevens will pun on the Latin meaning of "sorts": *sors, sortis,* fate. The sentimentalist believes that a whole range of fates—"all sorts of flowers"—may be chosen. But his counterpart, "The genius of misfortune," knows that true artists must be obsessed, and so the idealization of willed artistic making glides into the recognition that art, too, is part of that "evil in the self" which finds fault with the world's copiousness—"from which / In desperate hallow, rugged gesture, fault / Falls out on everything."

So the mind takes the place of the volcano as an agent of destruction—this is only fitting from the poet who will later write "The Poem That Took the Place of a Mountain." But it is important to remember, as canto XIV will remind us, that "Evil in evil is / Comparative." There are varieties of obsession, varieties of fateful willing. If Stevens makes it difficult to absolve the imagination of fault, he makes it considerably easier to see how the artist's need to impose his singular cosmos on us differs from the schemes of the dangerous monomaniacs, such as the revolutionary Konstantinov:

> the lunatic of one idea
> In a world of ideas, who would have all the people
> Live, work, suffer, and die in that idea
> In a world of ideas.

Victor Serge called Konstantinov "a logical lunatic," and Stevens added: "The politics of emotion must appear / To be an intellectual structure." But so must the politics of escape, as canto XII—"He disposes the world in categories, thus"—makes clear. The sophist who parses out the distinctions between a "peopled" and an "un-peopled" world ends by willing both worlds away, and then tries to rid himself of his own will:

> That knowledge
> Of them and of himself destroys both worlds,
> Except when he escapes from it. To be
> Alone is not to know them or himself.
>
> This creates a third world without knowledge,
> In which no one peers, in which the will makes no
> Demands. It accepts whatever is as true,
> Including pain, which, otherwise, is false.

The longer "Esthétique" goes on, the harder it becomes to see just what Stevens intends by "Mal," whether one defines it as pain, evil, or consciousness itself. Verse paragraphs begin to swell and so does the pinpoint of definition. The notorious elegy "How red the rose that is the soldier's wound" marks either the apex or the nadir of this magnified blurring of boundaries. Stevens' strategy in this canto is precisely the opposite of that in "The Death of a Soldier." The earlier poem isolates the fall of one soldier in a landscape which does not stop to mark his death; in fact, the poet himself barely seems to record the event. And yet by resisting all noticeable signs of grief, "The Death of a Soldier" does manage to design an austere memorial to the worth of one human life even in the absence of eschatological certitude. But here it is literally a mountain of deaths that Stevens confronts, "the wounds of all / The soldiers that have fallen." This is true anonymity. The vision of all these deaths, and "the indifference to deeper death" which they portend, move Stevens to posit a "mystical" fraternity of the slain. It is as if the boisterous fellowship of pagan sun worshipers in "Sunday Morning" were transformed into a shadowy, cultic choir:

> The shadows of his fellows ring him round
> In the high night, the summer breathes for them
> Its fragrance, a heavy somnolence, and for him,
> For the soldier of time, it breathes a summer sleep,
>
> In which his wound is good because life was.
> No part of him was ever part of death.
> A woman smoothes her forehead with her hand
> And the soldier of time lies calm beneath that stroke.

The transvaluation of the wound in this other dimension, this "high night," calls to mind Dante's portrayal of Manfred in the *Purgatorio*, smiling as he points to the wound that liberated him from life. But when Stevens writes that "his wound is good because life was," does he mean that *life* was good, or that life simply *was*, and is now over? I suspect the latter is the case, since we are dealing with a "soldier of time." Placed just below "life was" on the page, ending the next line, is "death," as if to show that even an ungainly substitution is preferable to the harsh finality of that word. But it is the final image of a woman smoothing her forehead, a gesture both erotic and death dealing (a "stroke"), which offers the most to meditation. Stevens has put the whole elegiac enterprise in question here, since we can never know whether the woman is meant as an emblem of remembrance or forgetfulness. Does the soldier now reside as a living memory in her mind—compare Yeats' "They but thrust their buried men / Back in the human mind again"—or is he smoothed out of even that minimal existence, the furrow of his grave now effaced forever? "That stroke" would become a kind of second death, an oblivion.

As the poem's other canto of outright elegy makes clear, "Esthétique du Mal" avoids rousing easy pathos in its readers. "Softly let all true sympathizers come" begins movingly, as Stevens makes the elegist's familiar gesture of disavowing poetic resource:

> Softly let all true sympathizers come,
> Without the inventions of sorrow or the sob
> Beyond invention. Within what we permit,
> Within the actual, the warm, the near,
> So great a unity, that it is bliss,
> Ties us to those we love.

But the next long sentence seems almost a willful destruction of mood, as dirge turns into oration and we are left to brood only upon the resourcefulness behind the choice of a word such as "selvages." Throughout the canto, a sympathetic or universal diction, a plain song, wars with more idiosyncratic speech. It is easy enough to see how Stevens mounts the rhetorical ladder from "Be near me, come closer, touch my hand," to "the damasked memory of the golden forms," only to drop softly at the end, in another imitation of the dying fall in "Sunday Morning," to "Before we were wholly human and knew ourselves." No sooner does Stevens invoke the "familiar," in line 6, than he makes it unfamiliar enough to warrant interpretation: "This brother even in the father's eye, / This brother half-spoken in the mother's throat." The rhetoric of repetition persuades us that men are brothers, that war is fratricidal, even as the logic of this filiation is explored in more mysterious terms. Perhaps we are brothers in that our fathers regard us in like ("even") terms, and our mothers call us in the same "half-spoken" words of endearment. A broader reading would take "even in the father's eye" as meaning equal in the sight of God, with the further possibility of naturalizing God as the sun. The mother might then stand for earth, "mother's throat" becoming a powerful trope for the grave, a figure that is made explicit in the late poem "Madame La Fleurie": "His grief is that his mother should feed on him." At the end of canto VIII, Stevens pairs "spoken" with "broken" in an ominous internal rhyme that confirms our tendency to misread "half-spoken" as "half-broken": "half-broken in the mother's throat." We are brothers, then, both under the sun and in the grave.

The counterpoint to this elegiac sense of fraternity comes into the poem with the appearance of Satan in canto VIII, instigator as he was of the first filial as well as sibling disharmony. Stevens' growing obsession with his own family's genealogy is well known, and his poems of the forties begin to present the family plot as part of a general tragic and fatalistic outline:

> It may be that one life is a punishment
> For another, as the son's life for the father's.
> But that concerns the secondary characters.
> It is a fragmentary tragedy
> Within the universal whole. The son
> And the father alike and equally are spent,
> Each one, by the necessity of being
> Himself, the unalterable necessity
> Of being this unalterable animal.

This note on the House of Tragedy, with its emphasis on Father and Son, reads like an epigram Nietzsche might have written on *Paradise Lost*. It also helps to explain the unmistakable allusion to *Hamlet* in canto VIII, where Stevens balances Miltonic and Shakespearean paradigms:

Phantoms, what have you left? What underground?
What place in which to be is not enough
To be? You go, poor phantoms, without place
Like silver in the sheathing of the sight . . .

Not only is Stevens linking Hamlet and Satan here, as if he were drawing up a genealogy of English tragedy, but he also conflates Hamlet and the ghost of Hamlet, Sr., in his evocation of a "phantom" for whom "to be is not enough / To be."

The esthetics of pain and evil lead inevitably to the poetic forms of elegy and tragedy. The more one reads Stevens, the more one recognizes him to be a supreme elegist—and the more elegiac much of his poetry is seen to be. Tragedy, as I have mentioned, becomes indistinguishable for him from fate or "necessity," as he calls it in canto XIII, and both terms almost become synonymous with heredity, the working out of the family curse:

This force of nature in action is the major
Tragedy. This is destiny unperplexed,
The happiest enemy.

Since Stevens is surely punning on "hap," it is redundant to call destiny "happiest." But the whole phrase is grimly felicitous, for "happiest enemy" captures two antithetical meanings: destiny is our most dangerous foe (on the presumption that a happy enemy is a bad sign), or our least dangerous (since it proves happiest for us). It all hinges on whether or not one "prefers" being destroyed from within: "One feels its action moving in the blood," which, as Stevens says elsewhere, has rather a classical sound.

For all this talk about the nature of tragedy, Stevens remains skeptical about the existence of the tragic vision in our time. His personae are most convincing when they face calamity alone, whereas tragedy requires some communal backdrop to lend it authenticity. It also requires communal belief in an ideology of some sort. The wittiest line in "Esthétique du Mal"—"The death of Satan was a tragedy / For the imagination"—dates the death of tragedy from the loss of belief, not in God, but in his chief adversary. Looking beyond this expiration, as he so often does, to the coming of a new order, Stevens sees the possibility of renewing the covenant of tragedy:

> The mortal no
> Has its emptiness and tragic expirations.
> The tragedy, however, may have begun,
> Again, in the imagination's new beginning . . .

By speaking so indefinitely of "the tragedy," Stevens deliberately intensifies the ambiguity of this hesitant prophecy. Are we to celebrate this sense of tragedy, do we require it in order to be human? Is it a mark of strength to face "the tragedy" with imagination?

An even deeper desire, both masked and unmasked by the poem's rhetoric, enters with this promise of a new beginning for the imagination. In cantos IX and X Stevens turns away from tragedy and elegy toward the oracular consolations of "chant," a word that comes as close as any other in his vocabulary to bearing the full weight of all that poetry can do: "we require / Another chant, an incantation, as in / Another and later genesis." The sound of this chant will be as the sound of "mighty waters," to use Wordsworth, though Stevens cannot avoid a slight touch of derogation in the self-consciously deepening voice which can find no more suitable verb than "bubbles up":

A loud, large water
Bubbles up in the night and drowns the crickets' sound.
It is a declaration, a primitive ecstasy,
Truth's favors sonorously exhibited.

These are waters in which the acedic poet who opened "Esthétique" might take his cure. Such a restorative baptism is predicated on the birth of the new or second self—that "later genesis."

No amount of study will ever produce consensus on the logic of transition in "Esthétique," but the poem does seem to drift from neurasthenia in the face of apocalyptic threat, through elegiac and tragic response (including the strong discovery of fate), to moments of near-prophecy such as the "return to birth" spoken of in canto x. (This is not the concluding stage, of course.) This delineation says nothing about the tonal and grammatical vagaries of "Esthétique du Mal," however, which often seem not only to work against, but to resist, the poem's own logic. The dry opening sentence of canto x—"He had studied the nostalgias"—obscures what the rest of the section makes clear: namely, the etymological and emotional force of nostalgia, "pain or grief for one's home." Home in this instance is the womb, the muse-mother being an odd caricature out of Dada or Toulouse-Lautrec: "the softest / Woman with a vague moustache and not the mauve / *Maman*." The pain or goad that drives toward this version of home is the promised recovery of desire, but in a "later" form which sublimates it into an urge "To accomplish the truth in his intelligence":

> His anima liked its animal
> And liked it unsubjugated, so that home
> Was a return to birth, a being born
> Again in the savagest severity,
> Desiring fiercely, the child of a mother fierce
> In his body, fiercer in his mind, merciless
> To accomplish the truth in his intelligence.

"Esthétique" opened on a note of exile, but here Stevens returns; the distance between self and home, bridged by "letters," collapses. The fierce compression of this passage, not to mention the apotheosis of the child, points ahead to "The Auroras of Autumn" or "The Owl in the Sarcophagus," where the connection between apocalypse and renovation is made explicit. "Being born / Again" is a violent act not far removed from annihilation; enjambment highlights the necessity of crossing a divide, and since stress falls on "Again" as much as on "born," we are left brooding on what form this second birth will take. The poetic return to origins—repetition with a difference—implicates past and future, so that in the lines quoted above Stevens begins in the past tense and ends with the infinitive. More dramatically, his carefully indeterminate (or logically illogical) phrasing makes it impossible to distinguish between child and mother. Is the child "fierce / In his [i.e., his own] body," or is it the mother inside *him*, in a daring reversal of nature, who inspires her son's ferocity? And yet Stevens needs just such a distinction, since earlier in the poem he rejected the paternal deity for the very reason that it was "over-human . . . not to be distinguished." In its place, as a possible way out of our dilemma, he set "the health of the world." Canto x gives us that health in the maternal shape of "the softest woman," latest avatar of the fat girl in "Notes toward a Supreme Fiction," who was herself a "mundo." In Stevens' conception, she is both an object of desire and the principle of desire itself.

At the end of this dense canto, Stevens invokes the concept of innocence, a theme that will return with greater majesty in "The Auroras of Autumn":

> It was the last nostalgia: that he
> Should understand. That he might suffer or that
> He might die was the innocence of living, if life
> Itself was innocent.

I will postpone a full discussion of what innocence might mean to Stevens until my reading of "Auroras." But it is worth noting that the term arises near the end of that poem as well, where it also proves to be something of a tempting but false conclusion. The very next canto of "Esthétique," after all, begins: "Life is a bitter aspic." As in "The Auroras of Autumn," innocence here becomes a desperate way of explaining nature's indifference to our total death. The volcano knows no pain, its unfeelingness also a sign that it has no malicious designs against us. More to the point, the power behind the volcano had no designs against us—indeed, has no designs at all, for such a power does not exist. This denial of intention to nature leaves a vacancy which is, precisely, reality itself. In the canto on Satan, Stevens once again makes us hearken to the first apprehension or sighting of this absence: "How cold the vacancy / When the phantoms are gone and the shaken realist / First sees reality." Fear then gives way to "the imagination's new beginning" and to the subsequent invention of a new myth to fill the void: the softest woman, reality. That this woman should also be called a mother indicates that the myth has its roots in the desire to be self-begotten: for to imagine one's mother is also a version of autogenesis, the romantic origination of self. (The latent pun in the final line of canto v, "Before we were wholly human and knew ourselves," surfaces at this point.) But Stevens soon regards this myth as only another attempt to explain reality, a nostalgia in the weak sense of the word. The energy brought into the poem by this imagined second birth dwindles into maternal consolation. At this point, we can recognize the confusion throughout between two opposed versions of innocence. In one, innocence means simply that nature is guiltless, while in the other, nature becomes a muse-mother who offers us understanding, but at the cost of weakening our sense of fate.

It is the business of the eleventh canto, an almost programmatically bitter one, to reestablish that sense without also bringing on an incapacitating fatalism. One way Stevens does this is by adopting the pose of the epicure, the "man of bitter appetite" who has a stomach for the absurdities lodged in pain and evil. The announcement that "We are not / At the centre of a diamond" dispels the nostalgias, as does the mordant wit that traces our fall in the drop of paratroopers:

At dawn,
The paratroopers fall and as they fall
They mow the lawn.

The epicurean speaker takes a kind of perverse delight in seeing the traditional figure of Death the Mower in the swath cut by the soldiers as they land. As he well knows, these men are mowers whose flesh is also grass. A faintly hysterical note creeps into this grim tableau with the Poe-like passage built upon the obsessive clamor of the bells, the bells:

> A vessel sinks in waves
> Of people, as big bell-billows from its bell
> Bell-bellow in the village steeple. Violets,
> Great tufts, spring up from buried houses
> Of poor, dishonest people, for whom the steeple,
> Long since, rang out farewell, farewell, farewell.

This is "evil made magic," in the words of "Extracts from Addresses to the Academy of Fine Ideas." Stevens feared the demon in him that could only too easily find the right esthetic perspective on any event. Even when the demon turns daemon, as in the famous rhyme "Natives of poverty, children of malheur, / The gaiety of language is our seigneur," the glibness of esthetic distancing remains a real danger. But the epicure is insatiable, and even his own magic soon palls. In a negating *ritornello*, he turns against his arrangements, preferring instead to taste the world's bitterness on his own tongue. This epicurean act of communion certainly owes something to Keats and particularly the "Ode on Melancholy," as Bloom points out,[7] for Stevens captures the Keatsian stylization of pleasurable pain:

> The tongue caresses these exacerbations.
> They press it as epicure, distinguishing
> Themselves from its essential savor,
> Like hunger that feeds on its own hungriness.

In the preceding canto the maternal myth "proved him against the touch / Of impersonal pain." Here such contact is cultivated, as if pain could be dispelled by homeopathic ritual. Instead, a solipsistic void is discovered beneath the mask of detachment—an extreme impersonality formed in reaction to the very heart of impersonal suffering.

Yet the epicurean esthete is still capable of embellishing the "hunger that feeds on its own hungriness" with heroic, if nihilistic, verbal gestures. When the adornment vanishes, as in the bleak canto which follows, a lethal plainness takes over, and the play of language turns into barren, sophistical juggling. Beyond impersonality lies the utter extinction of the will in its capacity to assert well-being, to differentiate between pain and health:

> the will makes no
> Demands. It accepts whatever is as true,
> Including pain, which, otherwise, is false.

These lines return us to the afflicted poet of the opening cantos and to the lines I suggested as his appropriate motto: "regard the invalid personality . . . without the will to power." Without the will there is no poetry. From this nadir, "Esthétique" must ascend to its final chant.

The movement whereby temporary eradication of the will serves only to insure its strong return is described by Poirier in "Writing Off the Self": "Since this is humanly intolerable, reductiveness is instead imagined as a sort of spring which, pushed down to a point where it touches the root nerve of the will, then recoils, projecting us into a creative upward movement which reconstitutes the self and the world.[8] Poirier accuses humanistic criticism of invoking "the trope of the processes of descent-ascent" in order to reinforce the poetic will and to keep the human image intact, even when the poet under question might want, for a number of reasons, precisely the opposite to occur. We need always to keep in mind Poirier's warning against the facile critical assumption that every gesture toward annihilation calls forth a corresponding act of restitution—even when it is Stevens himself who seems to recoil from the intolerable. After all, what critic would have dared predict how "Esthétique" soars in its final lines? In the space of one canto, Stevens seems intent on replacing malaise with health, impotence with power, despair with delight. The abruptness with which "the reverberating psalm, the right chorale" bursts upon us compounds the note of wonder in such expressions as "who could think," "who could have thought to make." True, there are hints throughout "Esthétique" of our need for a stronger voice, but the affirmations upon which Stevens closes, however colored by "dark italics," remain startling. The poem answers its own call, beyond expectation.

The whole of canto xv is spoken in what might be termed Stevens' common voice, the voice of "we." Distinguishing Auden's use of the first-person plural from Yeats's, Richard Ellmann writes: "When Auden uses the word 'we,' he means all humanity, while when Yeats uses the same pronoun he means a limited and elect community."[9] "We" means all humanity for Stevens as well, for as he put it elsewhere: "the whole race is a poet." Auden, of course, would never ground commonality on the romantic conception of a general poetic will; Stevens finds the idea not only legitimate but restorative. The final canto of "Esthétique" is a variant upon the thesis that "the health of the world might be enough," as Stevens surmised earlier in the poem. Now he adds to that world the people who live in it—restoring the destructive subtractions of canto XII—and especially their creations, their own "sensuous worlds." The twenty-four lines of the last section are evenly divided between the physical world and our perceptions of it. By declaring that "the greatest poverty is not to live . . . ," Stevens turns against the drift toward renunciation that has haunted the poem thus far. As in "Sunday Morning," paradise is seen as the realm of the bloodless, where life is lived in "the minor" key, to switch to the musical metaphor Stevens now uses:

> The greatest poverty is not to live
> In a physical world, to feel that one's desire
> Is too difficult to tell from despair. Perhaps,
> After death, the non-physical people, in paradise,
> Itself non-physical, may, by chance, observe
> The green corn gleaming and experience
> The minor of what we feel. The adventurer
> In humanity has not conceived of a race
> Completely physical in a physical world.
> The green corn gleams and the metaphysicals
> Lie sprawling in majors of the August heat,
> The rotund emotions, paradise unknown.

"Rotund emotions" belong to global men, embodiments of the world's health. "Paradise unknown" compresses into two words Stevens' long-running, occasionally satirical feud with orthodox accounts of the afterlife. Whatever difficulties one has with the notion of pure physicality, the portrait of the dead souls waiting to rise again at sound of the trumpet, only to find themselves "sprawling" under an unexpected blast, is Joycean in its cruel puncturing of spiritualist pretense. Modulation into the major is announced with fanfare by a couplet in which writing and voice are united.

> This is the thesis scrivened in delight,
> The reverberating psalm, the right chorale.

No longer is the sublime something one reads about between letters; the epistolary esthete is transformed into a scribal bard. Stevens has found a voice with which to sing in face of the mountain: Vesuvius becomes his Mont Blanc.

As psalmist, Stevens sings for the whole congregation, a role he adopts even more openly at the end of "The Auroras of Autumn." With monosyllabic precision, he probes the limits of isolated thought, giving the sole mind its due but acknowledging its incapacity to conjure up the world's particulars. "One might have thought of sight" sounds like Satan measuring himself against God, but the correction follows quckly along with the true note of wonder: "but who could think / Of what it sees, for all the ill it sees?" Miltonic diction, at least, survives in the menacingly easy glide of "all" into "ill," as if the world's fall were inseparable from its creation. (As with the Miltonic parody in canto IV, the wording is Milton's while the view of the Fall is closer to the romantics'.) Another string of monosyllables reckons the contribution of all the isolated acts of perception which go into the making of a whole—but a whole in which those parts are still visible:

> And out of what one sees and hears and out
> Of what one feels, who could have thought to make

So many selves, so many sensuous worlds,
As if the air, the mid-day air, was swarming
With the metaphysical changes that occur,
Merely in living as and where we live.

If obsessiveness bred by isolation is one of the principal sources of "mal," then these lines sing because a curse has been lifted. Malaise also loves company, even if the infinitive "to make" conceals the precise agent responsible for producing all these selves. Is Stevens celebrating the swarm of human creativity, much like Aeneas on the ramparts of Carthage, or is he admiring his own protean *oeuvre*? This passage bears some resemblance to the lifting of the mask at the end of "Credences of Summer" and the disclosure of the magus' personae. But "swarming" is also a word Stevens uses at the close of "An Ordinary Evening in New Haven," where it applies to the poetic will of the whole species (what Stevens calls "the general fidget"):

These are the edgings and inchings of final form,
The swarming activities of the formulae
Of statement, directly and indirectly getting at . . .

Again, the indeterminacy fostered by the infinitive allows Stevens to blend these created spheres, to subsume wonder at his own works within an overarching regard for the sum of human *poesis*.

But I have been avoiding the darker italics in the concluding passage. Stevens' buoyant tone and the replacement of fatalism by active creation make it easy to overlook the more somber note struck by this "swarming" activity. We can think back to the overt war poem of 1942, "Dutch Graves in Bucks County":

> Angry men and furious machines
> Swarm from the little blue of the horizon
> To the great blue of the middle height.

In 1944, merely by living as and where we live, we fill the skies with engines of destruction. Why fear the groaning of Vesuvius when man-made calamity is just overhead? But of course it is impossible to tell just what produces this agitation in the heavens at the end of the poem. For all we know, Vesuvius may finally have exploded. "Esthétique" begins just before noon—"It was almost time for lunch"—and ends in the air of midday. Perhaps the poem's interval has seen the volcano cease to threaten and actually burst, filling the air with its swarming debris.

Whether Stevens' auguries of apocalypse are inspired by natural or human violence, they raise the question of how we are to defend ourselves against threatened extinction. In other words, how do we survive? The delight Stevens discovers here at the close of "Esthétique" springs from his faith that we will come through; the whole poem is anchored on its last two words, "we live." And Stevens' refusal to close the poem with the interrogative that might have been called for is a further sign of his spiritual recovery, or belief in preservation. The well-known conclusion of "The Noble Rider and the Sound of Words" (1942), an essay much concerned with poetry's ability to resist and withstand a state of war, equates the imagination with survival:

> It [the mind] is a violence from within that protects us from a violence without. It is the imagination pressing back against the pressure of reality. It seems, in the last analysis, to have

> something to do with our self-preservation; and that, no doubt, is why the expression of it, the sound of its words, helps us to live our lives.[10]

The strategy for self-preservation upon which "Esthétique" finally settles is a little cannier than that of the prose passage. Instead of opposing force with force, Stevens seems to adopt an attitude of divide and conquer—divide the self, that is, in order to avoid being conquered by the violence from without. His vision of proliferating selves (near-homonym to "cells") and worlds amounts to a denial of our extinction; we cannot be eradicated if traces of us are present in everything we see and hear and feel. At most, we will suffer a "metaphysical" change, or exchange: a transformation into some form of life of which we are already a part, by virtue of our perceptions. As Helen Vendler says in another context, Stevens gives "credence to the plenty of the world as it is preserved not in the earth but in the mind."[11]

The occasion for Vendler's remark is an essay in which she demonstrates the career-long perseverance of Keats's "To Autumn" in Stevens' mind. Poetic survival, of course, is a powerful example of a metaphysical change which might be regarded as ameliorating death. Poetry is certainly part of the world's plenty, and for Stevens, Keats is almost a synonym for copiousness. At the end of "To Autumn," Keats traces his own escape route, sending his soul aloft with the gathering swallows, headed as they are for what Stevens called the "visionary south." The swarming Stevens sees at the end of "Esthétique du Mal" seems to mark a covenant of escape from the volcano's calamitous presence, as if Keats's gathering was now transformed into a more hectic swarm. In a poem so concerned with survival, it is only appropriate that a sign of one poet's survival in another should close the meditation.

By keeping poetry alive in a world at war, Stevens hopes to keep that world alive. His aim is not to preserve an image of the world through accurate mimetic representation, but to offer his deepest, most idiosyncratic sense of that world. We ward off destruction of our innermost selves by giving evidence of our continuing ability to feel. Poetry is the true home front, its war of words a vital propaganda. The winding paths of meaning in "Esthétique du Mal" are not evasions of the catastrophe at our back; they are necessary proof that one mind, at least, can still ply the difficult trade of metaphorical thought, even while realizing that time may be running out. Having once more proven to himself that he still exists as a poet, Stevens offers this example as testament to the mind's power to endure the violent reality of war.

2

Boreal Night: An Apocalyptic Reading of "The Auroras of Autumn"

> This sort of thing . . . makes me feel pretty much as a man must feel in a shelter waiting for bombing to start.
>
> In the autumn I badly need my mother, or something. This has always been the toughest time of the year for me.
>
> I cannot say that there is any way to adapt myself to the idea that I am living in the Atomic Age and I think it a lot of nonsense to try to adapt myself to such a thing.
>
> —*Letters of Wallace Stevens*

The greatness and the difficulty of "The Auroras of Autumn" arise from the same source: the poem has more overlapping spheres of reference, sustains a wider range of emotional intensity, than any other long poem of Stevens'. There is much that will always escape the interpreter of "Auroras," but little sense of evasiveness in the poem. Stevens' rhetoric here is both denser and more direct than in "Esthétique du Mal." The sense of immediate danger is heightened—as presiding image, the auroras are more active than the volcano—and the poet's presence in the scene is augmented. At the same time, this immediacy in no way diminishes the larger threat of apocalyptic violence. For if Vesuvius could waste "in solid fire the utmost earth," then the auroras' power is no less. Clearly, these lights induce a reaction that cannot be explained by recourse to the natural phenomenon alone. Late in the poem, Stevens will declare the auroras "an innocence of the earth," but this does not mean that they are to be regarded only as part of nature. What *is* their composition, then? This can be posed as a question of sources: from where did Stevens "get" the auroras? "Wherever he found the symbol, whether in literature, or in nature . . . ," writes Vendler;[1] I would suggest adding history to the list, as perhaps the deepest motivation of all. For, I would argue, what triggered the finding of the auroras by Stevens was not so much a text as an event: the dropping of the atomic bomb, the epitome of all the great explosions prefigured in the volcano's trembling. For just as Stevens could read the volcano as an ancient figure for present calamity, so the auroras merged old and current versions of apocalypse in a dense textual weave. When the books are about to burn, the values they radiate are brightest.

To say that the aerial violence of the war figures crucially in the constellation of meanings represented by the auroras is probably to invite skepticism on the part of even the best readers of Stevens, who, while having long ago abolished for themselves the myth of his emotional detachment, would nonetheless resist any suggestion of topicality where only dark sublimity or generalized *angst* might reign. And yet, "Auroras" is recognized as a poem relentlessly grounded in presentness: "the confrontation of the present is insisted on over and over . . . the eye is not allowed to stray."[2] Even though the poem was written in 1947, the end of the war, not to mention visions of the end produced by the war, can still be considered part of the present. Wherever Stevens might have found the auroras, he would not have had to look far for the source of a phrase such as "gusts of great enkindlings" (canto II), or for the image of a world "on flames." Of course Stevens uses all the rhetorical resources of the apocalyptic tradition (an odd phrase), but these are reimagined, reinvested, through his own sense of being witness to the present moment's threat. As he faces that crisis, Stevens calls into play every aspect of his own poetic arsenal, a career's worth of strategies and stratagems, for the potential destruction of civilization brutally mocks his effort to bring that career to completion.

Apart from the question of multiple referents for the auroras, there is the disturbing issue of their relationship to us—or, rather, the relation we find within us to this emblem of destructive force. Are we to say, along with Yeats: "Whatever flames upon the night, / Man's own resinous heart has fed"? On the other hand, the poem loses much of its force if the auroras are read only as natural signs. The lights glide across all sorts of boundaries between the human and nonhuman, now appearing as something created by us, now appearing alien. The poem's deepest conjectures have to do with the union between human destructiveness and nature's power, as well as the extent to which creativity is implicated in violence. Its deepest pathos arises from Stevens' desire to find a saving innocence in the imagination. Yet there is also a sense in which the poem moves toward a possible transcendence of the vulnerable network of earthbound relationships. For the last canto of "Auroras" speaks of a "never-failing genius" who "lived all lives that he might know," but leaves the object of such knowing unnamed. The importance of this omission is underscored by the fact that every other use of "to know" in the poem refers to knowledge based on familiarity. In canto IX, the brothers "knew each other well"; in canto VII, as Stevens imagines the extinction of our planet, he reflects on how the evidence that "We knew each other well" is sure to be lost. Only a reading of the whole poem can begin to explore what Stevens has left so enigmatic at the end.

And yet, "Auroras" proceeds to its large-scale truths through the narrow corridors of one room, one house, one family. The destruction of the House is an ancient principle of tragedy, and Stevens at times resembles an Aristotelian commentator in his assessments of tragic causality:

> A cabin stands,
> Deserted, on a beach. It is white,
> As by a custom or according to
>
> An ancestral theme or as a consequence
> Of an infinite course.

By 1947, the year in which "Auroras" was written, Stevens' brothers and sisters were dead. His best friend, Henry Church, died on Good Friday of that year. His father had died in 1911, his mother a year afterward: in the words of the poem, "The house will crumble." On its most personal level, "Auroras" mourns the dissolution of the poet's family, before rising to consider the undoing of us all. As an elegy for the vanishing of one house, it should be compared to another poem written just after the war, Frost's "Directive." Although Frost seems concerned primarily with the house of his marriage and his own implied guilt in its destruction, "Directive" is not without its sense of universal calamity either, as indicated by the terse sentence summing up the fate of those quaint "village cultures": "Both of them are lost."

Just how deeply the loss of family is felt by Stevens can be illustrated by a turn, fittingly enough, to a possible early source of the description of the mother in canto III. Genetic explanations have almost no value for the interpreter of Stevens, but this may be a unique instance. When, at the opening of canto III, the poet chants, "The mother's face, / The purpose of the poem, fills the room," he is saying something momentous about poetic origins and ends, but he may also be remembering how he had felt thirty-five years before, as he watched his mother dying. Stevens recorded his feelings in journal entries for June 25 and July 1, 1912, and it is fascinating to place these words alongside the rendering of the mother's "second" death in "Auroras." They yield a number of details bearing upon the poem and also give us an early glimpse into Stevens' lasting stoic temperament. It would be three more years, with the writing of "Sunday Morning," before Stevens achieved as mature a vision in his poetry; indeed, the arguments against paradise in "Sunday Morning" take on even greater poignance when read as a continuation of Stevens' meditation on his mother's "expectation."

From the journal entry for June 25, 1912:

> Her present sickness has aged her more than many years; and when I saw her a month ago she was much whiter than I had expected. When I went home, I saw her sleeping under a red blanket in the old blue-room. She looked unconscious.—I remember very well that she used to dress in that room, when she was younger, sitting on the floor to button her shoes, with everything she wore (of summer evenings, like these) so fresh and clean, and she herself so vigorous and alive.—It was only a change for her to be in the blue room. . . . Fortunately for mother she has faith and she approaches her end here (unless her mind is too obscured) with the just expectation of a re-union afterwards; and if there be a God, such as she believes in, the justness of her expectation will not be denied. . . . She would play hymns on Sunday evenings and sing. I remember her studious touch at the piano, out of practice, and her absorbed, detached way of singing. . . . The house is a huge volume full of the story of her thirty-five years or more within it.[3]

On July 1, Stevens adds:

> She had a good night, Sunday night. In the morning, before I left, she saw what a bright morning it was and remarked on it. She said that she would like to have "a room right in it." She was propped up. She would not lie down until after I had gone. . . . She wishes not to complain. She said that she had had her "boys" and asked, "Do you remember how you used to troop through

> the house?" After all, "gentle, delicate Death," comes all the more gently in a familiar place warm with the affectionateness of pleasant memories.[4]

I would like to remain a while longer in the precincts of the family romance. The dominant colors (or blanknesses) that strike the eye in these journal entries are remarkably similar to those in the second canto of "Auroras": white, red, and blue. But now it is the son who has whitened, the son who prepares to lie down amid "blue-red sweeps." And it is the son, later in the poem, who wishes to have a "room right in it," even though he recognizes the room to be situated "In hall harridan, not hushful paradise." These journal entries can help us to grasp the convergence of personal, poetic, and political forces in "Auroras." For example, the ellipsis marking the transition from the idea of solitude governing canto II to the mother's face in canto III represents a divide that can only barely be bridged by reason, though "the man who is walking," prophetic Son of (Wo)Man that he is, may cross from poetic to natural origins by admitting that the "different" whiteness he tries to find again in canto II—the biologically spotless, poetic origins embodied in a poem such as "The Snow Man"—collapses before the primary pallor of the dying mother's face, now his own. The white "flowers against the wall" in canto II are more than "a kind of mark": they are a mark of kind, a revelation of mortal kinship leading to the superimposition of the mother's face upon the son's. Origins and ends mingle throughout "Auroras," as one might expect from a poem dominated by the serpent of indiscriminate beginning and end.

Throughout the poem, Stevens makes the auroras as difficult to define as he possibly can. Are they natural phenomena, or do they "stand in" for some human creation? As they slither through the sky, these lights simply cannot stop signifying. Even if we regard them as evidence of the way in which human catastrophes such as the Second World War contaminate our perception of nature—the auroras as "fallout"—the question of their natural status still remains. Does the Bomb release a power already in nature, and if so, what kind of power is that? Bloom identifies Stevens' first idea of nature with the sun, but after the explosion of the first atomic bomb, Einstein is reported to have said: "For the first time in history men will use energy that does not come from the sun."[5]

The auroras first appear as a sign in the heavens, for which Stevens ventures a number of different interpretations in the dense opening canto:

> This is where the serpent lives, the bodiless.
> His head is air. Beneath his tip at night
> Eyes open and fix on us in every sky.
>
> Or is this another wriggling out of the egg,
> Another image at the end of the cave?
> Another bodiless for the body's slough?
>
> This is where the serpent lives. This is his nest,
> These fields, these hills, these tinted distances,
> And the pines above and along and beside the sea.
>
> This is form gulping after formlessness,
> Skin flashing to wished-for disappearances
> And the serpent body flashing without the skin.
>
> This is the height emerging and its base . . .
> These lights may finally attain a pole
> In the midmost midnight and find the serpent there,

In another nest, the master of the maze
Of body and air and forms and images,
Relentlessly in possession of happiness.

This is his poison: that we should disbelieve
Even that. His meditations in the ferns,
When he moved so slightly to make sure of sun,

Made us no less as sure. We saw in his head,
Black beaded on the rock, the flecked animal,
The moving grass, the Indian in his glade.

At least four discrete visions of the auroras can be made out: (1) they are a sign of a guardian demon watching us, or "fixing us"; (2) they image a rebirth into a new age, thus explaining why the second tercet is filled with end signs, primitive warnings of apocalypse; (3) they point to a Creator, not merely a demon, a "master of the maze of body and air"; and (4) they point to their origins in nature, to the earthly serpent, "the Indian in his glade."

Throughout the opening canto, Stevens writes with extreme discrimination of matters that cannot, after all, be discriminated. Vendler points to the relentless present-tense grounding of the poem, indicated by all the pronouns.[6] But such specificity is undone by the invisibility of the serpent whose head is air. "Head" is an interesting word in this context; it is as if Stevens can tolerate a bodiless serpent but not a headless one. Yet no sooner does Stevens declare the serpent to have a head, than he retracts that characterization and terms the head a "tip." Alongside this, the potentially ominous image of eyes opening and fixing upon us seems, if not benevolent, then at least concerned. The real question here at the opening of "Auroras" has to do with what sort of mind lies behind the eyes. Coloring that question is the sinister opening assertion—"This is where the serpent lives"—and the feeling we gather from it that where the serpent lives, it is not quite possible for us also to live. The poem's second tercet focuses upon the vessels or containers of the serpent—cave, egg, body's slough—all of which it manages to break and escape from. It is no surprise to discover that this gnomic creature is rather more indestructible than the earth upon which he nests, but it is disturbing. By contrast, the snake at the close of canto I is a natural creature, evoked through memory, who was part of a privileged moment of esthetic perception. The snake's slight movement as he "made sure of sun" struck the poet and made him no less assured of his own imaginative response to nature. Stevens turns against the master of the maze by seeing again, in memory, the nonmalevolent serpent in the glade. A natural vision such as this celebrates the nonapocalyptic imagination. And yet Stevens may banish that idea as soon as it is invoked, since the next canto begins: "Farewell to an idea."

> Farewell to an idea . . . A cabin stands,
> Deserted, on a beach.

Given the fact that Stevens is bidding adieu, it is surprising that canto II is written in the present tense. Never before has Stevens put quite such weight upon the ellipsis, although it is a constant feature of his style. As will also be true later on in "The Rock" ("The sounds of the guitar were not and are not . . . Absurd"), there is considerable doubt whether the ellipsis marks a break with the preceding thought or a reinforcement of it. "A cabin stands, / Deserted," conjures up a different sense from that of mere emptiness; it suggests recent occupancy, even flight, perhaps. Coming upon a "deserted" scene, one encounters something of the same perplexity Keats displays in "The Fall of Hyperion."

It is white,
As by a custom or according to

An ancestral theme or as a consequence
Of an infinite course. The flowers against the wall
Are white, a little dried, a kind of mark

Reminding, trying to remind, of a white
That was different, something else, last year
Or before, not the white of an aging afternoon,

Whether fresher or duller, whether of winter cloud
Or of winter sky, from horizon to horizon.
The wind is blowing the sand across the floor.

The sequence leading from "custom" to "ancestral theme" to "infinite course" works itself back in time, to a potential source or origin. (I am assuming that an ancestral theme would predate a custom.) The dry, white flowers, a "kind of mark" serving as a reminder, are like bookmarks, trying to hold a sense of place. Stevens is representing himself as fumbling in his memory, reminding himself, trying to remind. What he seems to be searching for is an earlier, more powerful version of whiteness, such as he had discovered in "The Snow Man," or in the returning afternoons of "The Poems of Our Climate." This, however, is an aging afternoon. Just how weak Stevens' sense of weather has become is shown by the pun on weather itself: that great source of power for Stevens is turned into the quibbling conjunction "whether." The grand gesture of the Arabian moon in "Notes," who "throws his stars around the floor," now becomes the ominous scattering of "The wind is blowing the sand across the floor." Remnants of power do remain, however, in the span of a phrase such as "horizon to horizon."

To return to the phrase which governs the canto: "Farewell to an idea." Stevens' intention to keep the nature of this idea ghostly is indicated, first, by his use of the indefinite article, and then by his refrainlike repetition of the phrase over the next two cantos. The same question may be asked of "Farewell to an idea" that was put to Stevens' use of the ellipsis: does it apply to what precedes or follows in the poem? The words themselves, both "Farewell" and "idea," can lead us to Florida, by way of "Farewell to Florida" and "The Idea of Order at Key West." And since the closing tercet of canto I was situated in a Floridian landscape, Stevens may be saying adieu to the Floridian idea yet again. "Farewell to Florida" began with the image of a snake shedding its skin upon the "floor"; at that point in Stevens' career, such an image could indeed serve as an emblem of change or rebirth for the self. But now the serpent is aloft, a master of the maze. "Farewell to Florida" also involved a turn toward the north, exactly the direction canto II will take. The phrase "Farewell to an idea" collapses both of the early poems together, and it makes us reflect that they were each addressed to a muse, the muse of Florida.

A comparison of "Auroras" with "The Idea of Order at Key West" is also instructive, since once again Stevens is striding the beach—but now there is no singing girl to behold, nor is there any companion, even a pale Ramon, to share the vision. Most intriguingly, there is a dazzling light show presented by each poem. At the end of "The Idea of Order at Key West," the vision of lights was a comforting sign, an esthetic vision of order, a sign of romance:

> The lights in the fishing boats at anchor there,
> As the night descended, tilting the air,
> Mastered the night and portioned out the sea,
> Fixing emblazoned zones and fiery poles,
> Arranging, deepening, enchanting night.

There is no sense of enchantment to the "fiery poles" Stevens now espies in the heavens:

> With its frigid brilliances, its blue-red sweeps
> And gusts of great enkindlings, its polar green,
> The color of ice and fire and solitude.

From fiery poles to polar green, the sense of enchantment has cooled, because the vision of the heavens ablaze is no longer a *trompe l'oeil* produced by the poet's urge to see the zodiac in the sky as a sign of the enduring romance tradition. Now the lights truly are there; the sublime lights are literal. Part of the dread produced by the vision of the auroras, or whatever they signify, is the dread involved in seeing a fantasy come alive.

"The Idea of Order at Key West" takes place "as night descended"; the equivalent moment in "Auroras" comes toward the end of the second canto: "A darkness gathers though it does not fall / And the whiteness grows less vivid on the wall." "A darkness" sets this particular darkness apart from any purely naturalistic context, for which "darkness" alone would have sufficed as description. It is hard to tell whether the refusal of darkness to fall is indeed a comforting event: the gathering darkness seems more ominous than the mere falling of night. The crossing between stanzas conspires to keep this darkness aloft. (Notice that Stevens cannot any longer make out the shape of a flower against the wall; it is now simply a question of whiteness.) The whole world seems in the process of being reduced to black and white, which makes the light display at the end of the canto all the more sinister or commanding. At this point in "Auroras," Stevens reads his prophecy in the very absence of writing on the wall—the blank wall, the blank sand, the blank page.

Stevens has been threatened by such annihilation before. In "The Snow Man" he gathered power from the threat of extinction, practicing the accomplishment of an extremist in an exercise. The Floridian sand also proved a threat to the very existence of personality, but "Farewell to Florida" managed to escape "the bleaching sand." Canto II of "Auroras" is written by a survivor, but a survivor who realizes that the apocalypse is not far off. "Gusts of great enkindlings," after all, is a phrase that has great resonance in 1947, capturing the aerial terrors of the recent past as well as prefiguring a greater fire next time. After all, ice and fire traditionally vie for the honor of ending the world, bringing on the "solitude" Stevens refers to at the end of the canto. To borrow Frost's grim flippancy over such matters: "Some say the world will end in fire, / Others in ice."[7]

So canto II presents us with two contradictory interpretations of "Farewell to an idea": first, it may be read as an adieu to the Floridian vision of the muse. Second, it also seems to renounce the idea behind the wintry scene, namely that by reducing the sphere of perception to the bare minimum—"the whiteness grows less vivid on the wall"—a compensating rush of power will arise. How to choose between the two, except to say that Stevens seems on the verge of losing everything, even as his poetic power gathers itself for one final effort. What Stevens says of the beach—"the long lines of it grow longer, emptier"—might be said of the kind of writing he is aiming for in this canto, a poetry which bespeaks effort. In this vein, many of the lines are end-stopped, appropriately enough for a career that itself seems on the verge of becoming end-stopped.

The next appearance of the refrain "Farewell to an idea" is, if anything, even more mysterious. "Farewell to an idea . . . the mother's face" is an extraordinary statement. The transition or ellipsis is especially intriguing, since one might expect the mother's face to be precisely what Stevens is bidding farewell to, rather than what arises after such a valedictory gesture. The mother's countenance becomes an image of presence, not absence, and instead of disappearing, fills the room. Not only the mother's face, but "the purpose of the poem" fills the room as well. What, then, is Stevens saying farewell to, if he is in possession of the mother's face and the purpose of the poem? (By the end of canto III, the mother will be dissolved, but in the opening tercet she is unquestionably an image of presence. Indeed, at the opening of the tercet, she seems to be the very last thing Stevens has, and when she disappears he is truly bereft.)

Whatever idea Stevens says farewell to must have been something that kept him from the mother's face, and also obscured the purpose of the poem—in other words, a mask of some sort. The idea may have been simply that poetry could disguise its own origin and end. Only when that idea breaks down, or trails away in ellipsis, can dread be overcome and the mother's face confronted. Even the face of the muse—in Stevens' case the Floridian muse—veils the mother's countenance.

The discovery that the mother herself can be destroyed is a heightened version of the ancient topos of the muse's inability to protect her offspring. The mother "has grown old"; her failure to protect her children is best illustrated by the fact that she seems to fall asleep before they do:

> Boreal night
> Will look like frost as it approaches them
> And to the mother as she falls asleep
> And as they say good-night, good-night.

As in "The Waste Land," "good night" is a mark of how truly late it is.

On this great night, Stevens tells us that there will be "none of the prescience of oncoming dreams," which seems to promise a present repose, but might have more ominous meaning if the mother is indeed a higher muse. For she would be a muse without foreknowledge, a muse unable to know or guarantee the future. In short, she would be a muse who could not ensure fame, survival, literary immortality, and so Stevens declares that "the books will burn." The mother gives transparence to the present moment, but does not ensure visibility after death. Stars are an image of just such immortality, but Stevens says that they are beyond reach:

> The house is evening, half dissolved.
> Only the half they can never possess remains,
>
> Still-starred.

If what remains is beyond possession, what possibility exists for achieving transcendence?

For a poet of such luxuriant imagination, Stevens has always been drawn to images of poverty when attempting to portray the condition of the human race. One thinks of the tramp at the close of "*It Must Be Abstract*," or, later on in "Notes," Canon Aspirin's Cinderella-like sister. But the most striking of these emblems of pathos, it seems to me, comes at the close of canto III of "Auroras," when Stevens imagines the human family—fatherless, it would appear—huddled in a kind of makeshift bomb shelter, or place of hiding suitable for the refugees we have all become. But the refuge is discovered; there is a "knock like a rifle-butt against the door." Much human suffering is encapsulated in this wrenching image of the shelter being invaded. The father is gone, perhaps already dead. (On the biographical level, Stevens' father did indeed die before his mother.) The manipulation of perspective throughout "Auroras" is extraordinary, but never more so than at this point, where Stevens juggles so many levels of meaning at once, so many senses of the idea of the human family. The threat of annihilation comes to him as man, as poet, as member of the human race on the verge of destruction.

The fourth canto of "Auroras" belongs to the father, and it is one of the oddest things that Stevens ever wrote. Once again, there is the intoned "Farewell to an idea," only now "Farewell" seems a positive gesture: "Farewell to an idea . . . The cancellings, / The negations are never final." It is as if the first two farewells referred to ideas that preceded the poem, while now it is the idea of this poem that Stevens intends. The act of saying farewell takes on a restorative function; it seems as if the father's strength will suffice, for the father is "strong in the bushes of his eyes." Vendler notes the resemblance of those "bushes" to the burning bush,[8] and one might also compare them to "the lasting visage in a lasting bush" of "Notes." On the most human level, the bushiness of the father's eyes shields them from making contact with others, and reinforces the father's outsized distance from his son. The father appears, at first, to be another of Stevens' many rigid statues, impervious to change. Unlike the mother, who has been internalized in time, the father remains an outward projection in space. He "sits" as a judge is said to sit. It is worth remarking that although one might expect him to be a protective figure, he is not inside the shelter of the mind with the rest of the family in canto III. He seems, indeed, massively irrelevant. His function as judge or statuesque oracle is described in odd terms: "He says no to no and yes to yes. He says yes / To no; and in saying yes he says farewell." These are opaque lines, and the only sense I can make of them is that the father's voice, unlike his rigid countenance, is internalized in much the same manner as the voice of the superego, a voice synonymous with conscience. His "no" is equal to the no of conscience, his "yes" the sign of approval. Therefore, when he is imagined to contradict himself, to give approval where the superego says no, he vanishes, at least in this particular aspect. And it does indeed seem as if this rigid version of the father disappears once his role as forbidding policeman of the ego is banished. For just as there is more than one serpent in the opening canto, so there is more than one father in canto IV.

In his next avatar, the father suddenly becomes a grand leaper; breaking the statuesque mold, he suddenly "measures the velocities of change." This more active version of the paternal principle seems like one of God's good angels:

> He leaps from heaven to heaven more rapidly
> Than bad angels leap from heaven to hell in flames.

The father shares this quality of leaping with the auroras themselves, or rather the imagination *behind* the auroras, as Stevens will describe it in canto VI. No critic has yet remarked on the resemblance of the father to that enthroned imagination, but it is in the text and it is disturbing: "It leaps through us, through all our heavens leaps." Stevens addresses the father in prayer, using much the same language as he will later use in describing the auroras' "crown and diamond cabala":

> Master O master seated by the fire
> And yet in space and motionless and yet
> Of motion the ever-brightening origin,
>
> Profound, and yet the king and yet the crown,
> Look at this present throne.

What can Stevens mean by speaking to the father in much the same terms he will use to paint the auroras as symbol of the grim imagination? For Stevens seems to ascribe no malice to the father in canto IV; the father is hardly accused of "extinguishing our lives," to anticipate the charge made against the intelligence behind the auroras. Stevens does, however, grant the father all the accoutrements of the sublime imagination:

> He assumes the great speeds of space and flutters them
> From cloud to cloudless, cloudless to keen clear
>
> In flights of eye and ear, the highest eye
> And the lowest ear, the deep ear that discerns,
> At evening, things that attend it until it hears

The supernatural preludes of its own,
At the moment when the angelic eye defines
Its actors approaching, in company, in their masks.

Cantos III and IV repeat the structure of the Canon Aspirin cantos in "Notes," in which the Canon's sister and her children were presented first, followed by the canon soaring aloft in his angelic aspect, then descending to the children's bed. The father in "Auroras" is the same sort of ghostly guardian, however remote he appears from the scene of the threat.

The danger Stevens runs in using the same sort of language to describe both the father and the auroral imagination is one he wishes to run: namely, the danger of implicating the poetic imagination, as embodied in the father, along with the "grim imagination" symbolized by the auroras. This is a danger he will court in all of his late poetry, where the creative violence of the poetic mind is set beside the violence in nature and human nature. Can we say that the poet is innocent of these destructive tendencies?

Since this portrait of the father is couched in something of a childlike frame of memory, there remains, as Vendler points out, a comic dimension to it.[9] Bloom stresses the affirmative nature of the paternal figure,[10] and both he and Vendler downplay the father's power. The father does seem something of a cartoon character; but like the firecat in "Earthy Anecdote," he appears playfully omnipotent, a deflector of danger. The childlike fantasy of the omnipotent, paternal imagination will dwindle into the present reality of "the scholar of one candle" (parodic counterpart to "the master seated by the fire"), although the magus figure will return at the end of the poem in the guise of the rabbi. Why Stevens should wish to include this touch of the comic in the center of the poem is unclear, nor can the canto be pleasing to many readers. There is more than a touch of foolishness in this portrait of the undependable, chimerical father who cannot sit still long enough to be of real help to his children. What is most fascinating is the way in which Stevens blends regressiveness and sublimity in this portrait of the poetic principle. But at this point in "Auroras," the resort to magic will not work, nor will the use of surrogate selves, masks, mottled characters. "This present throne" is too powerful even for the kingly father.

Cantos IV and V get progressively more idiosyncratic, as Stevens allows himself wide indulgence in private patterns of meaning. The mode of poetic logic in these cantos becomes deeply associative, deliberately drifting off the path of clear argument. Understanding the difficult fifth canto, in particular, requires us to supply the hidden referent or springboard to action. The canto seems to sketch a series of bizarrely disconnected actions, but I believe they do coalesce into what Stevens calls "curious ripenesses / Of pattern in the dance's ripening." The canto begins innocently enough, but by its end Stevens will allow the words and lines to dribble down into nonsense.

Many actions are fused together in the fifth canto: some kind of ritual or feast seems to be taking place; the mother graciously "invites," while the father, in his raucous American way, "fetches." If we only remember the title of the poem, then we will have some clue to these proceedings, for if this is "Autumn" then we are witnessing a kind of harvest celebration. If we are guided instead by "Auroras," then Stevens is probably playing off the resemblance to fireworks—in other words, to a Fourth of July celebration, back in a time when colored lights in the sky signified joy, when rockets were toys. The canto indulges in deliberate regression, combining historical folksiness with blurred memories of one's own "folks," one's parents. As Stevens moves further backward in this canto he leaves behind the present meaning of the auroras, especially their figuration of the last war's destruction. But nostalgia soon turns to disgust, as the primitiveness of the ritual and Stevens' own sentimentality begin to overtake him. What began as a festival ends as a decadent extravaganza:

> We stand in the tumult of a festival.
>
> What festival? This loud, disordered mooch?
> These hospitaliers? These brute-like guests?
> These musicians dubbing at a tragedy,
>
> A-dub, a-dub, which is made up of this:
> That there are no lines to speak? There is no play.
> Or, the persons act one merely by being here.

Ritual has turned into aimless frenzy: Stevens seems suddenly to view the scene with adult eyes again, and what he sees is a new primitivism that has nothing folksy about it. The decadence of our days testifies to the kind of despair which overtakes societies gripped by apocalyptic fears.

The father's efforts to script the scene, to turn impending catastrophe aside with a show, dissolve as did the mother's touch. The severe dismissal, "There is no play," may be aimed elsewhere, namely at Yeats's "Lapis Lazuli," as if Stevens were intent on dismissing both high and low theater in the face of apocalypse. Yeats, of course, counsels us to keep the show going, to keep up the heroically gay pose even as the bombs fall:

> All perform their tragic play,
> There struts Hamlet, there is Lear,
> That's Ophelia, that Cordelia;
> Yet they, should the last scene be there,
> The great stage curtain about to drop,
> If worthy their prominent part in the play,
> Do not break up their lines to weep.

To this, Stevens replies: "the persons act one merely by being here." Tragedy comes merely in living as and where we live. Stevens may be taking a further dig at Yeats—at least at this point in the poem: the closing canto will take Yeatsian "gaiety" more seriously, by bringing in his clumsy musicians who go about "dubbing at a tragedy." "Lapis Lazuli," of course, closes with the soothing, if mournful, melodies of the serving man who "Carries a musical instrument." Against Yeats's "Accomplished fingers begin to play," set Stevens' "the musicians make insidious tones, / Clawing the sing-song of their instruments." The strictures of Yeatsian ritual demand that actors keep their lines intact. But what if "there are no lines to speak"? What if our actors are left "dubbing at a tragedy"?

Canto VII of "Auroras" begins with as enigmatic a reference as the "Farewell to an idea" cantos: "It is a theatre." Whatever "it" intends, whether the auroras or the globe of the earth, an elevated perspective is invoked, as if Stevens were rising to behold the full dimension of his theme. Something of the psalmist's tone of wonder enters into a line such as "And mountains running like water, wave on wave."

As the description continues, it becomes even clearer that Stevens is using terms that are synonymous with the powerful workings of the imagination. There is more than a touch of envy to the descriptions, as the auroral imagination is seen to fulfill perfectly Stevens' own prescription that, for example, "It Must Change":

> It is of cloud transformed
> To cloud transformed again, idly, the way
> A season changes color to no end,
>
> Except the lavishing of itself in change.

It also fulfills another obligation of the Supreme Fiction, namely that "It Must Give Pleasure":

> Splashed wide-wise because it likes magnificence
> And the solemn pleasures of magnificent space.

The auroras display a lavish imagination, one that is almost insulting by human standards. As in the final stanza of "A Postcard from the Volcano," light is smeared on the scene. But the most telling indication of the way Stevens views the auroral imagination comes in the line "The cloud drifts idly through half-thought-of forms." First of all, there is the hidden allusion to Keats's description of poetic power in "Sleep and Poetry": "might half slumbering on its own right arm."[11] In this case, idleness or slumber is a token of power. The word "drifts" is also revealing. Describing the way in which the poem moves through its sections, Stevens says: "What underlies this sort of thing is the drift of one's ideas."[12] Thus Stevens defines the auroras in terms of praise drawn both from Keats and from his own repertory, since "drift" is one of those characteristic words of understatement—"merely" is another—

which Stevens uses to signify power. In talking of "the drift of one's ideas," Stevens seems to imply that these ideas can acquire a life of their own, or drift away, and in this sense the dangerous drift of the auroras becomes a facet of Stevens' own imagination.

The sense of verticality that we find in "Auroras," as Stevens both lifts and lowers his eyes, is especially striking in the sixth canto. Much can be learned about the poem simply by following Stevens' gaze along this axis. At the close of canto I, for example, Stevens regained a sense of natural covenant and, perhaps, poetic identity by lowering his gaze to the ground and the merely natural snake upon it. Canto II followed a different strategy: when Stevens turned from the man who was walking and gazing blankly on the sand, to the "great enkindlings" in the sky, he retrieved a sense of power. Much of the pathos and frivolity brought into the poem by the parental images were banished with one quiet glance at the lights in the sky. So even if the auroras do represent a possible threat of annihilation, they are at times to be preferred to the happenings on earth. They represent power, after all, and sometimes power is preferable to pathos.

In canto VI, Stevens seems almost ready to worship the auroras or, better yet, ready to adopt the sublime perspective, the aerial view. Such a view rises above all human pain and sees history as "theatre." The problem, however, is that there is no plot; history, from this height, merely changes "the way / A season changes color to no end." Once again, the apocalyptic theatrics of Yeats are slyly undercut:

The theatre is filled with flying birds,
Wild wedges, as of a volcano's smoke, palm-eyed
And vanishing, a web in a corridor

Or massive portico. A capitol,
It may be, is emerging or has just
Collapsed. The denouement has to be postponed . . .

Stevens' scenario focuses on the birds scattering from the site of ruin, just as an earlier Yeats poem, written in the aftermath of the First World War, augured apocalypse from the panicked reaction of birds to the stirring sphinx: "all about it / reel shadows of the indignant desert birds." On the naturalistic level, Stevens' birds are responding to the coming of winter; but on a deeper level, their migration is a kind of transmigration, as they aim "palm-eyed" toward what "Sunday Morning" called "the visionary south." For these collapsing capitols, Stevens' version of the falling towers of "The Waste Land," foretell the death of a civilization.

The ellipsis after "the denouement has to be postponed" marks the end of Stevens' flirtation with worshiping the auroras. He puts an end to drift, and stages a quixotic charge against the forces of annihilation:

This is nothing until in a single man contained,
Nothing until this named thing nameless is
And is destroyed. He opens the door of his house

On flames. The scholar of one candle sees
An Arctic effulgence flaring on the frame
Of everything he is. And he feels afraid.

"Nothing" flaring on the frame of "everything"—if anything, the use of "nothing" in these lines is even more difficult to understand than in "The Snow Man." From the natural point of view, the auroras are simply loose, unbounded energy, good for "nothing" until contained in some human vessel or conduit. The process of internalization will be expounded fully in "An Ordinary Evening in New Haven":

> to say of the evening star,
> The most ancient light in the most ancient sky,
>
> That it is wholly an inner light, that it shines
> From the sleepy bosom of the real, re-creates,
> Searches a possible for its possibleness.

The evening star, however, does not threaten to extinguish us. The real question for the interpreter is whether to read "nothing" as signifying "negligible" or "nothingness." To take it as meaning "negligible" would be to emphasize the contest throughout the poem between Stevens' poetic sublime and the sublime of nature; the poet's quest would be to say of auroras and evening star alike that they are "wholly an inner light." To read "nothing" as nothingness, or perhaps negativity, deflects the poem in quite different directions. In this context, "nothing" has the force of annihilation, whether actively (through apocalyptic violence), or through the nihilism of evil. When it is a question of incorporating the natural power and beauty of the auroras, it is clear why Stevens wishes to internalize them. More intriguing, however, is the willingness he shows to contain their annihilating violence, their ability to destroy capitols. (Again, in a statement such as this, I am treating the auroras in more-than-natural terms. Throughout the poem, Stevens not only keeps the visible auroras in mind, but also foregrounds the difficulty of looking at these spectral lights and thinking of them *only as* lights.) The wish to contain their violence repeats the credo expressed at the close of "The Noble Rider and the Sound of Words":[13] "It is a violence from within that protects us from a violence without." The issue, once more, is one of self-preservation.

The unlikely figure upon whom this task devolves is "the scholar of one candle." Only Stevens could locate heroism in the gesture of opening a door—even upon such a night as this, when the whole world is on fire:

> He opens the door of his house
>
> On flames. The scholar of one candle sees
> An Arctic effulgence flaring on the frame
> Of everything he is. And he feels afraid.

By the end of the poem, the scholar will become a figure of greater largesse: "a vital, a never-failing genius." But here he remains a monkish figure, a beacon of light in a dark age. His last candle seems society's as well, the last flicker of civilization.

The series of assertions that mark the sixth canto give way to the rhetorical questions of canto VII, and once again seasonal metaphors for the imagination come to the fore. As long as we construe summer and winter in merely natural terms, we will be inclined to identify Stevens with the sort of imagination that "in the midst of summer stops / To imagine winter." But the imagination or the mind that Stevens portrays in this canto is larger than that encompassed by a natural context. The enthroned imagination of canto VII exists both in and out of nature. It is more than a *counter*-natural imagination capable of projecting itself into a later season; rather, it resembles the greater sky of "Anatomy of

Monotony": "over the bare spaces of our skies / . . . a barer sky that does not bend."

As canto VII proceeds and the notes of resemblance between poet and auroras mount, we may be forgiven our growing apprehension. Which side is Stevens on? Is he celebrating the enthroned imagination because it is like his own? Describing the mind behind the auroras as "the white creator of black, jetted / By extinguishings," brings its activity directly into the zone of writing. But midway through the canto, as if in reaction to this act of identification, Stevens rediscovers the communal frame of reference, lost to some degree since the first canto:

> It leaps through us, through all our heaven leaps,
> Extinguishing our planets, one by one,
> Leaving, of where we were and looked, of where
>
> We knew each other and of each other thought,
> A shivering residue . . .

The serpent feeds on destruction and thrives on worship; in moving toward the communal, Stevens poisons the serpent again, as in the first canto, by withholding belief in his power to extinguish *us*. For the satanic goat-leaper threatens to bring about the end of our solar system, "our planets," ushering in a cosmic ice age that dwarfs the seasonal metaphor of wintry death.

The last two stanzas of canto VII have been called the most surprising in all of Stevens' poetry,[14] as the auroras are deflected from what seems to be their mission of extermination; suddenly, they are said to be bent on their own destruction:

> But it dare not leap by chance in its own dark,
> It must change from destiny to slight caprice,
> And thus its jetted tragedy, its stele

And shape and mournful making move to find
What must unmake it and, at last, what can,
Say, a flippant communication under the moon.

"It dare not" lies somewhere between statement and proscription; similarly, "It must change" almost compels us to read, "It must be changed." The issue involved in saying that the auroras are turned away from destiny's straight path—or veer on their own account—has something to do with Stevens' wish to see the serpent's tip as a head in the opening canto of the poem. Where there is a head there is intelligence; the same may be said for the presence of "slight caprice." Why Stevens should want to find intelligence in precisely this place is unclear. The real point here is that Stevens refuses to tolerate the notion of a blind destiny, just as at the beginning of the poem he insisted that we were being watched by "eyes." Now he insists, further, that the intelligence behind the auroras is driven to discover its necessary antagonist—namely, us. The auroras are a force in search of a counterforce, tyranny in search of resistance. They can also be seen as celestial script in search of an earthly echo: "jetted tragedy" describes the flow from the instrument of writing, while "stele" plays on *stilus*, the writing instrument itself. "Stele" is, of course, also the surface upon which writing is engraved: a monument, often a grave marker. So this "jetted tragedy" may amount to an epitaph in search of a survivor to behold it.

The final line of canto VII demonstrates Stevens' prescription for survival—a blend of canniness and irreverence. "Say, a flippant communication under the moon" brings together several antithetical meanings. On the one hand, a flippant communication hardly seems an adequate act of rebellion or refusal. And yet, flippancy is the opposite of worship, as well as a human response to the weight of the preceding argument—a weight graphically illustrated by the column of lines (the "stele") resting upon that mock-heroic gesture at the bottom of the page. (Canto VII begins with an image of enthroned imagination and ends in the sublunary realm.) "Say" seems more flippant yet, a disconcerting interjection, or throwaway, at this crucial point in the poem. But its placement at the beginning of the line, and the comma following it, give pause. Suppose one were to read "say" as a strong imperative, as in "Say, Muse!" If the rest of the line were given its full weight, "under the moon" would become "under the sign of the moon," just as "caprice," a few lines earlier, leads to the sign of capricorn, the "goat-leaper." If we are indeed under the sign of the moon, then we are in the region of lunacy—of the divine sort special to poets. "Say, a flippant communication under the moon" is both an outrageous reduction, and preservation, of poetry's divine madness. In Stevens' characterization, poetry is the antithesis of tyranny, since it mocks itself and all authority as well. The muse responds to Stevens' flippant call.

Canto VIII involves anything but flippant communication. The emergence of innocence as a theme might appear anomalous, but I think that the apocalyptic situation accounts for Stevens' effort to find a place or a time free of guilt. When Stevens says, "There is never a place" (for innocence), he seems to be ruling out the idea of utopia, except that utopia already means "no place," and thus takes into account the hypothetical nature of its own construction. "There is never a place" does not rule out utopian vision. Stevens does, however, give priority to the time of innocence, its place in the memory or in the future projection of the mind. One might compare Stevens' grid of time and place with that of an overtly apocalyptic poet such as Blake. In the Jerusalem hymn, for example, Blake finds both a time and a place for innocence: "ancient time," "Jerusalem." Blake fuses the utopian, or forward-looking, aspect of apocalyptic thinking with its restorative dimension; Jerusalem was built in ancient time and, hence, will be built again. It is very difficult to know whence Stevens derives his "time of innocence." It does seem mostly to come from memory—the innocent mother, the warmth of family feeling, the rendezvous with the beloved. Beneath memory lies instinct, and Stevens is willing to associate the idea of innocence with what he terms "the sense against calamity":

> If it is not a thing of time, nor of place,
>
> Existing in the idea of it, alone,
> In the sense against calamity, it is not
> Less real.

Such a sense becomes a basis for our instinctual resistance to the pressure of outward violence, a forceful retaliation by the ego.

In "Notes," a calmer poem, Stevens allowed more latitude to the possible existence of the "Supreme Fiction":

> It must be visible or invisible,
> Invisible or visible or both:
> A seeing and unseeing in the eye.

But when it is a question of innocence he grows more insistent, if not more convincing:

> It is like a thing of ether that exists
> Almost as predicate. But it exists,
> It exists, it is visible, it is, it is.

Considering the overwhelming visibility of the auroras, it takes courage for Stevens to insist that innocence is *visible*, as if he were directly contradicting the evidence of his eyes.

What are we to make of the easy victory Stevens seems to win over his own fear, when he discovers that the auroras are after all merely natural phenomena?

> So, then, these lights are not a spell of light,
> A saying out of a cloud, but innocence,
> An innocence of the earth and no false sign
>
> Or symbol of malice.

To say that the lights are only lights may be to admit that one cannot see beyond their natural surface. The tonality here is one of relief, as if Stevens were glad of no longer being able to frighten himself with visions; but the loss of ability to see those visions, those spells, means trouble for the poet, and must also mean a certain disappointment on the reader's part, who hungers after some greater meaning for the auroras. In other words, to dismiss the auroras as Stevens does here is to come dangerously close to dismissing the poem's prime area of tension. What kind of prophet declares the danger past, the threat to be only innocent?

It is also important to notice that no sooner does Stevens utter the word "innocence" than he modifies it to "an innocence of the earth." In "Esthétique du Mal," as we saw, Stevens spoke of nature's indifference to our deeper death, and then asked if life itself was innocent, as if to imply uncertainty as to whether nature's innocence meant an absence of intention. In "A Prayer for My Daughter," Yeats begins by speaking of "the murderous innocence of the sea," but at the end of the poem invokes a concept he calls "radical innocence":

> Considering that, all hatred driven hence,
> The soul recovers radical innocence
> And learns at last that it is self-delighting,
> Self-appeasing, self-affrighting,
> And that its own sweet will is Heaven's will.

Between "an innocence of the earth" and "innocence" lies something of this distinction between guiltlessness, or lack of intention to harm (which can nevertheless kill), and true innocence. Yeats's version, of course, involves the ability to free oneself from guilt; the strong, solipsistic soul blesses itself and aligns itself with heaven's will.

It still might seem odd to readers that Stevens should invoke the auroras at a historical moment when they are bound to appear natural analogues for human destructiveness, to describe them in ways that only further the resemblance, and then declare the auroras to be a part of natural "holiness." His point in making the comparison and then trying to break it may be to insist that there is still a version of natural power uncontaminated by man. More important, in the aftermath of the war, is the corollary assertion that there are still "natural" forms of death. The scenario of the children lying down, to sleep or to die, is especially moving. If it is death they face, then they do so in a way that was not possible for so many in the last war. They die with dignity, treating death as holy. Stevens' wording is very precise here:

That we partake thereof,
Lie down like children in this holiness,
As if, awake, we lay in the quiet of sleep.

Stevens presents an intensely human ambiguity in these lines. "As if, awake, we lay in the quiet of sleep" might mean that we are children who pretend to be asleep at this moment; we are really awake, only pretending to be asleep, in order to trick our mothers. Stevens says that we mimic the "quiet" of sleep, not the "peace" of that state—to invoke terms from "The Owl in the Sarcophagus." Although Stevens uses the image of children feigning sleep, the scene has Stoic overtones of a willing acceptance of death. We assume the pose of death at the end, as we wait to be overtaken by the real thing.

Canto VIII ends by pushing the notion of nature's innocence over the line separating it from radical innocence, by invoking the image of the mother playing a lullaby for her children on her accordion. Is this the poet's privilege, to be sung asleep?

As if the innocent mother sang in the dark
Of the room and on an accordion, half-heard,
Created the time and place in which we breathed.

By the end of the poem, Stevens will have banished this idea of the mother's responsibility for our songs, but here he is tempted to Wordsworthian reveries on the role of the maternal presence in his own songs. One should turn, for comparison, to the passage in Book I of *The Prelude* where Wordsworth realizes the force of his nurse's songs, wed to the sounds of the river Derwent, in his own poetic birth.[15] At this moment in "Auroras," Stevens seems to be turning away from the scene of his death as a man and as a poet, and returning instead to the scene of his birth into a music meant only for him. "Breathed," the last word of the canto, is crucial in this regard, since it can serve as a figure for poetry. Stevens is trying to bring round the sphere, to draw a circle around his life as a poet by tying together the moment of life and the moment of death, the moment when he first learned how to breathe and the moment when he breathed his last—both presided over by the muse-mother.

The ellipsis between cantos VIII and IX is the most natural in the poem, a true gliding connection with little hint of disjunction. The ease with which Stevens moves from poetry-as-breath to the thought of others reveals the communal basis of his plural pronouns:

> the time and place in which we breathed . . .
>
> IX
>
> And of each other thought—in the idiom
> Of the work, in the idiom of an innocent earth,
> Not in the enigma of the guilty dream.

"Idiom" does not lead to idiosyncrasy here, but to "the work," to "an innocent earth." The casting out of guilt reminds one of Yeats's self-cleansings. Yet "the enigma of the guilty dream" is not only a private act of self-accusation, for "enigma" points to the very act of prophetic fortune-telling Stevens seems to engage in throughout much of "Auroras." It is precisely in "the enigma of the guilty dream" that the fortunes and fears of our race seem to lie, and for the moment Stevens is quite willing to let the enterprise of interpreting the riddle subside. An image of his brothers returns; it is the very image that, according to his journal, his mother had used on her deathbed, capturing the comradeliness of the fraternal troop:

We were as Danes in Denmark all day long
And knew each other well, hale-hearted landsmen
For whom the outlandish was another day

Of the week, queerer than Sunday. We thought alike
And that made brothers of us in a home
In which we fed on being brothers, fed

And fattened on a decorous honeycomb.

Stevens' family was Dutch, and Denmark stands to Holland in much the same way that the New Haven of "Ordinary Evening" stands to Hartford: in Harold Bloom's formulation, a place that is not home, but close enough to home.[16] Stevens' boyhood coincided with the last two decades of the nineteenth century, a period he always regarded as a particularly fat and peaceful one, a time in which nothing outlandish had yet happened. Once again, Stevens turns against his own images of consolation and nourishment, regarding the comfort of that period as a cowardly retreat from the rigors of fate.

No portion of "Auroras" is more daring in its sharp transitions than the middle section of canto IX. Beginning with "This drama that we live," Stevens switches frames of reference as abruptly as he will do anywhere in his poetry. With the notion of "drama" we return to the theater of the mind, the attempt to place the events in the sky within a framework of pageantry:

This drama that we live—We lay sticky with sleep.
This sense of the activity of fate—

> The rendezvous, when she came alone,
> By her coming became a freedom of the two,
> An isolation which only the two could share.

The understated formulization of "Esthétique"—"Merely in living as and where we live"—now becomes a drama. Stevens counterpoints it with a vision of the brothers bundled together in sleep, cuts back to the present moment, "the activity of fate," and then, in one of the most emblematic and private of his privileged moments, offers the moment of rendezvous with the beloved as an antidote to fate. The swing between origins and ends in this passage can be seen, most simply, as a passage between freedom and fate. The rendezvous is an erotic covenant to be matched, perhaps, with the natural covenant offered by the vision of the sleeping snake in canto I, whose movements "made us no less as sure." At their inception, these covenants seemed to promise assurance and freedom, but gradually they are revealed to be only instruments of fate. "This drama that we live" is presented here through Stevens' technique of overlapping beginnings and endings.

This meditation on origins and ends results in a brutal return to the mode of prophecy and apocalyptic urgency. "Shall we be found hanging in the trees next spring?" Stevens asks. "Of what disaster is this the imminence: / Bare limbs, bare trees and a wind as sharp as salt?" The vision of the postwar landscape in these lines is strikingly close to Beckett's in *Godot*. Suicides, of course, were found hanging in the trees by Dante in hell, and although suicidal moments are not what we expect to find in Stevens, there may be some suggestion that the "isolation" which only the lovers can share might culminate in suicide. Indeed, in this postwar landscape of desolation, the whole race seems on the verge of killing itself. Nor is it just our perverse desire to injure ourselves that we must fear, for the powers of the sky are after us as well: "The stars are putting on their glittering belts." The stars seem to be girding for Armageddon, "a great shadow's last embellishment." In elegies, the poet's fate is often bound up with the stars, to whose realm he is assimilated at the end of life. From his earthly perspective Stevens can regard this onset of Armageddon only with trepidation. This is the apocalyptic moment proper, celebrated so often by Yeats, both early and late. Throughout *The Wind Among the Reeds*, for example, Yeats sighs for the time that must pass before he can be united with his beloved. That moment will arrive only after the apocalyptic dissolution of all earthly barriers. "He Hears the Cry of the Sedge" puts it forcefully:

> I wander by the edge
> Of this desolate lake
> Where wind cries in the sedge:
> *Until the axle break*
> *That keeps the stars in their round,*
> *And hands hurl in the deep*
> *The banners of East and West,*
> *And the girdle of light is unbound,*
> *Your breast will not lie by the breast*
> *Of your beloved in sleep.*

By saying that "The stars are putting on their glittering belts," Stevens tells us that they are coming to get him, but for good or ill? Is he to be assimilated to their ranks, along with the great poets? Of his own greatness as a poet, Stevens was not in doubt. So the real question is what is lost in this process of "stellification."[17] Whether the lovers are to be suicides or victims of another's violence, Stevens sees no afterlife for them. There is no sense that after apocalypse will come the true erotic life. And yet, although he is willing to see the rendezvous end, he cannot quite regard the final parting word as part of nature's innocence:

> It may come tomorrow in the simplest word,
> Almost as part of innocence, almost,
> Almost as the tenderest and the truest part.

Here, the iterations of "it is" from the previous canto, meant to assert the existence of innocence, subside in the face of death, to "almost, almost."

Canto IX, particularly, highlights the vertical axis of the poem, with its movement from "the idiom of an innocent earth," to the pair "hanging in the trees," to "The stars . . . putting on their glittering belts" and, in a tonal descent at the end of the canto, back to the hushed tones of earth and innocence—"the tenderest and the truest part."

"An unhappy people in a happy world" at first glance does not seem to be the most promising of Stevens' aphorisms. Stevens is writing simply, but his words have great dialectical weight. First, there is the matter of attempting to close a poem of the complexity of "Auroras" with a "summing-up" phrase, an epigram or aphorism. In an article by Susan Sontag on Roland Barthes, there is the following aperçu about the nature of epigrammatic thinking: "It is the nature of aphoristic thinking to be always in a state of concluding; a bid to have the final word is inherent in all powerful phrasemaking."[18] So the imagination is always at the end of an era, always about to conclude. Stevens has ended a number of his long poems prior to this with some vision or statement of happiness; "It Must Give Pleasure," the final section of "Notes," held true to its word and gave us emblems of pleasure or enjoyment:

> there is an hour
> Filled with expressible bliss, in which I have
> No need, am happy, forget need's golden hand,
>
> . . . .
>
> I can
> Do all that angels can. I enjoy like them,
> Like men besides, like men in light secluded,
>
> Enjoying angels.
>
> . . . .
>
> And we enjoy like men, the way a leaf
> Above the table spins its constant spin,
> So that we look at it with pleasure.

"Esthétique du Mal" ends with "the thesis scrivened in delight." And "Credences of Summer" closes with a vision of the author's characters enjoying a "youthful happiness":

> Complete in a completed scene, speaking
> Their parts as in a youthful happiness.

Of course, in this vision happiness belongs to the author's works, not to the inhuman author himself. To appropriate the language of "Auroras," the characters are part of the "happy world," for as personae they avoid the fate of "an unhappy people." Fate is a good word here, since Stevens is surely punning on "hap," as he did in "Esthétique" where "destiny unperplexed" was called "the happiest enemy." We are an "unhappy" people primarily because we are unlucky, or ill-fated. The world *is* fate, so it is almost tautological to call it happy.

Now, "happy" seems like a particularly weak word from which to wring so many declensions. Yet Keats, for one, talks openly of happiness throughout the Odes. For him, we are also "An unhappy people in a happy world." His struggle in the Odes is one of attempted identification with the ground of that happy world. The happy world for Keats in the Nightingale Ode is centered on the bird's natural artistry: "too happy in thine happiness." In "Ode on a Grecian Urn," the realm of happiness has much more to do with the world of the artifact, the made thing, "All breathing human passion far above." Those who think Stevens leans too heavily on the slender word "happy" should reread the third stanza of the "Ode on a Grecian Urn":

> Ah, happy, happy boughs! that cannot shed
>   Your leaves, nor ever bid the spring adieu;
> And, happy melodist, unwearied,
>   Forever piping songs forever new;
> More happy love! more happy, happy love!

The happy world is the world of nature or the artifact, "Complete in a completed scene."

In "Lapis Lazuli," Yeats also follows Keats by assigning "gaiety" to the world of the artifact, whether on stage with Hamlet and Lear, or on the lapis lazuli itself. "Their ancient, glittering eyes, are gay," Yeats says of the Chinamen on his "urn." Yeats's strategy is to make the reader forget he is writing about an artifact. The last six lines of the poem are written from within the frame, as it were. Yeats has also subtly included himself in the scene by means of a brilliant use of enjambment just preceding the final six lines. He has set himself "There" in the blessed space of gaiety:

Though doubtless plum or cherry-branch
Sweetens the little half-way house
Those Chinamen climb towards, and I
Delight to imagine them seated there;
There, on the mountain and the sky,
On all the tragic scene they stare.
One asks for mournful melodies;
Accomplished fingers begin to play.
Their eyes mid many wrinkles, their eyes,
Their ancient, glittering eyes, are gay.

In the third line in this passage, Yeats includes himself, by means of enjambment, along with the Chinamen: "Those Chinamen . . . and I." Only the next line tells us that he is imagining them already arrived at their destination. (Notice how Yeats intervenes with his own imagination to place the figures on the carving.) His "delight" becomes one with their own gaiety. They are all in a happy world of Yeats's own device. That world is "there," not here. Yeats's "There" is the esthetic antidote which Keats found on the urn or with the nightingale in embalmed darkness, antidote to the equally strong "here" of "Here, where men sit and hear each other groan."

But Stevens, although he has followed his personae, his angels, into that sanctum of delight in other poems, chooses at the end of "Auroras" to enforce the distinction between an unhappy people and a happy world. "In these unhappy he meditates a whole": the emphasis at the end of "Auroras" is not on the creator's delight, his happiness in his own personae's happiness, but on his unhappiness. This has nothing to do with the loss of poetic vitality. Any doubt that Stevens might have shown at the beginning of the poem about his own powers is dispelled in the image of the master:

> The vital, the never-failing genius,
> Fulfilling his meditations, great and small.

Paying homage to his own powers always leaves Stevens a little nervous, and he is careful to accentuate the tricksterlike or confidence-man side to his poetic disposition. He is "the spectre of the spheres, / Contriving balance to contrive a whole." His more solemn counterpart is the rabbi, whose role it is to "solemnize the secretive syllables," to attend to the congregation: "Read to the congregation, for today / And for tomorrow, this extremity." What is significant here is Stevens' faith that there will be a tomorrow, though much of the poem seems doubtful of that. The rabbi seems to be something of an intermediary between Stevens and the congregation; by solemnizing the secretive syllables, he makes them accessible.

And yet the rabbi is also a token of faith, an emblem of continuity for Stevens. He comes by surprise, as if materializing into the poem—another contrivance of the maguslike spectre of the spheres. Partly, he materializes to answer the prayer of 1930 in "The Sun This March": "Rabbi, rabbi, fend my soul for me, / And true savant of this dark nature be." As an early and important emblem for Stevens, his reappearance marks a continuity with an earlier poetic self and a partial appeasement of the elegiac motto "Farewell to an idea." But to invoke the rabbi just after the end of the Second World War is a far different gesture from that of the earlier poems. It is altogether in keeping with Stevens' reticence that he should simply name the rabbi and let it go at that, but anyone who has closely followed the poem's argument and anxieties cannot, I think, feel that the figure is arbitrary or merely intratextual. The rabbi, of all souls, can now say: "An unhappy people . . ." And yet the congregation is still there and, what is more, will be there tomorrow.

The breeziness with which canto x opens begins to disappear as the poem winds down. And the poem does literally wind down—to a little "nick." So much can be made out of the last line, however, that to call it a reduction from the grand panoply of the poem's opening seems a mistake. As the poem—and his poetic life—begin to near a conclusion, Stevens reflects on the "whole" he has meditated. In a curious claim for himself, he asserts that he has "lived all lives"—a bit like Eliot's Tiresias saying "I, Tiresias, have suffered all, foreseen all":

> In these unhappy he meditates a whole,
> The full of fortune and the full of fate,
> As if he lived all lives, that he might know.

Everywhere else in "Auroras," as I mentioned at the beginning of this chapter, "know" refers to familiarity, which is not surprising considering the place of the family in the poem. But here the object of "know" is left dangling. Can one "know" all lives? Is there a knowing beyond our lives, beyond our earth even? The last question becomes especially appropriate when we move to the end of the poem. Stevens seems to move in the direction of reducing the import of the poem, diminishing its contest to "a haggling of wind and weather." Even more astonishing is the poem's final line. Our last vision of the auroras comes in a simile; they are "Like a blaze of summer straw, in winter's nick." Again, it seems as if Stevens is deliberately narrowing the field, the scope, of his poem, in much the same way as at the end of "Credences" he brought us to the meadow late at night to find the inhuman author meditating there with the goldbugs. But just as the meadow in "Credences" might also be seen as the meadow of the heavens, the goldbugs as stars, so there is the same tendency here toward outrageous shrinking and expansion. This is both straw and the whole of our fields; this is both a local fire and the final holocaust or apocalypse. The apocalyptic reading has a corollary, not surprisingly, in Yeats, one which goes to show once more the differences in how each beheld our possible end. Yeats' "In Memory of Eva Gore-Booth and Con Markiewicz," a poem that says at every turn, "Farewell to an idea," a poem that shows "a raving autumn shear[ing] / Blossom from the summer's wreath," ends with the following clarion call to apocalypse:

> The innocent and the beautiful
> Have no enemy but time;
> Arise and bid me strike a match
> And strike another till time catch;
> Should the conflagration climb,
> Run till all the sages know.
> We the great gazebo built,
> They convicted us of guilt;
> Bid me strike a match and blow.

For Yeats, the end of time is precisely what the scholars wish to know. It seems, indeed, to be the end or aim of their knowledge. For the Stevensian scholar of one candle, this blaze "that he might know" is less joyous an occasion, since Stevens is uncertain as to what he might know in that blaze.

And yet there might indeed creep into Stevens' lines a touch of Yeats's eagerness to see the end. But for Stevens, always, there is the sense that such knowing will mark the end of familiar knowing, the end "of where we were and looked." As remarkable as these speculations, however, is the matter of Stevens' perspective in these lines. Where has he ascended to, that he can see the world go up "Like a blaze of summer straw, in winter's nick"? Has he indeed become one with the stars, overlooking the whole scene?

There is also the microcosmic dimension to reckon with, the dimension of pathos. For that blaze can also be read as a simple, futile fire, a last piece of summer stockpiled against the bite of winter ("winter's nick"). The fire seems to burn in a cave of winter and, as such, it reminds one of the fool's words upon the heath: "Now a little fire in a wild field were like an old lecher's heart—a small spark, all the rest on's body, cold." Farewell to an idea. And yet Stevens calls the flame a blaze, not simply a fire, and if one does not wish to take the blaze as a macrocosmic, final conflagration, it would after all be a warming fire, a firing-up again, a rebirth. Indeed, it might be a blaze to rout the serpent from his lair "in winter's nick."

3

Poems of Peace: "Credences of Summer" and "An Ordinary Evening in New Haven"

He is the theorist of life, not death.

Canto XXIV of "An Ordinary Evening in New Haven" (1949) helps to situate the poem's historical moment. This canto locates itself in a "clearing," both temporal and spatial, set "at the edge of afternoon," just after some vaguely specified act of violence:

> The consolations of space are nameless things.
> It was after the neurosis of winter. It was
> In the genius of summer that they blew up
>
> The statue of Jove among the boomy clouds.
> It took all day to quieten the sky
> And then to refill its emptiness again,
>
> So that at the edge of afternoon, not over,
> Before the thought of evening had occurred
> Or the sound of Incomincia had been set,

There was a clearing, a readiness for first bells,
An opening for outpouring, the hand was raised:
There was a willingness not yet composed,

A knowing that something certain had been proposed,
Which, without the statue, would be new,
An escape from repetition, a happening

In space and the self, that touched them both at once
And alike, a point of the sky or of the earth
Or of a town poised at the horizon's dip.

Without allegorizing too blatantly, I think we can equate the moment when "they blew up / The statue of Jove" with the war; more interestingly, Stevens declares the violence to have been part of "the genius of summer." Probing further, if we think of "the neurosis of winter" as referring to the ice age of the Depression thirties—and Stevens' poems of the thirties are filled with images of wintry rigor mortis—then we can see why Stevens should be compelled to speak of a "*genius* of summer" and link that to the war, since only the dark genius of human destructiveness, it would seem, could have broken the icy spell of the Depression. "An Ordinary Evening in New Haven" places itself in the aftermath of destruction, in the quiet clearing. But it remains conscious throughout of the apocalyptic fears which preceded it; in other words, the poem is shadowed by "The Auroras of Autumn." In the complex interplay between "Ordinary Evening" and "Auroras," we see the full range and complexity of Stevensian self-revision, for the sky which Stevens seeks "to quieten" is the flaring night sky of "Auroras." To some degree, that poem's sense of dread, its fears for the survival of our earth, are not laid to rest until "Ordinary Evening." It took four years from the war's end for Stevens to write his poem of peace. As the pairing of this chapter suggests, I also see "Credences of Summer" as a postwar poem of the "clearing," as well as a poem engaged in an analogous act of revision—in this case, directed toward "Esthétique du Mal." My readings of both "Ordinary Evening" and "Credences" concentrate on these processes of revision, as Stevens (and the world of which he was part) recovers from war and the anxieties it spawned.

"Credences of Summer," composed in 1946, celebrates the first full summer since the end of the war. We should not be surprised that its portrait of a peaceful summer day is shadowed from the beginning by a dark countersong, nor that Stevens becomes the latest poet to discover the significance of *et in Arcadia ego*. The summer day itself might be capable of obliviousness, but the poet who looks out on the land knows that the graves are shallow:

> Now in midsummer come and all fools slaughtered
> And spring's infuriations over and a long way
> To the first autumnal inhalations, young broods
> Are in the grass, the roses are heavy with a weight
> Of fragrance and the mind lays by its trouble.

It would not be difficult to proceed through the whole of "Credences," showing the presence of what Helen Vendler has called its "elegiac and brutal claims for the land's ripeness."[1] Vendler does not link the undersong in "Credences" to the war, appealing instead to Stevens' temperamental preference for change, even violent change, over the *longueur* of stasis. But surely the ephemerality of peace and the dark encroachment of death can also be traced to the difficulty of believing that a *state* of peace has arrived, as opposed to an interval. After all, Stevens' most formidable vision of a state of war, "The Auroras of Autumn," was written a year after "Credences," two years into the peace. Only with "An Ordinary Evening in New Haven" does Stevens put violence to rest.

If the poem's carefully structured "fall" into night's disembodiments makes it clear that Stevens intended this peace to be provisional, then it ought to be equally apparent that he has also succeeded in momentarily stilling the day. Such moments of what Stevens calls "arrested peace" lie at the heart of the poem and should be read against corresponding moments of apocalyptic anxiety in "Esthétique du Mal." "Credences of Summer" works to heal some of the wounds uncovered in "Esthétique": it is a poem of recovery even more than of peace. And one of its prime recoveries is the idea of "natural" death, as opposed to the catastrophic death brought about by the volcano. The sense of an ending pervades "Credences," but by and large Stevens manages to make that sense appear to be harmonious with desire, a fulfillment rather than a disruption. Peace brings back the possibility of dignified death, or "good death," to use the phrasing from "Extracts from Addresses to the Academy of Fine Ideas":

> It is death
> That is ten thousand deaths and evil death.
> Be tranquil in your wounds. It is good death
> That puts an end to evil death and dies.

As both "Extracts" and "Esthétique" make clear, the evil death of total war also involves a poisoning of the very ground on which we live, so that the recovery of "good death" and the curing of the ground go hand in hand. To some degree, the cure depends on a change in perception; as the necessary angel might say, one must "see the earth again . . . Cleared of its stiff and stubborn, man-locked set." The pastoral vision of "Credences" retains the elegiac tinge so often assumed by the genre, and manages to see death as occurring within the bounds of nature, rather than as transgression:

> One of the limits of reality
> Presents itself in Oley when the hay,
> Baked through long days, is piled in mows.

This emblem of natural process should be compared with its antithetical image in "Esthétique du Mal," the vision of the paratroopers who "mow the lawn" as they land, and who are soon to be mown down themselves. But now the natural innocence of a phrase such as "piled in mows" has been recovered from the verbal corruption of war. The poem's best example of such recovery comes in the description of the tower in canto III as "Axis of everything, green's apogee // And happiest folk-land." In addition to hymning the land, Stevens also celebrates the return of "axis" and "folkland" to the lexicon of sanity. After this example, he can go on to call the Ecclesiast of "Ordinary Evening" the "axis of his time."

But the most telling revision wrought upon "Esthétique" by the later poem centers on the crucial image of the mountain. In the second canto of "Credences," volcanic fire is internalized and transformed into the searing power of the eye intent on burning away falsehood:

> Let's see the very thing and nothing else.
> Let's see it with the hottest fire of sight.
> Burn everything not part of it to ash.

The primary mode of "Credences," however, does not involve turning violence from within against violence from without. Its processes are gentler, in accord with the diminution of external threat; reality, no longer wounding, can now be absorbed rather than warded off. At the least, Stevens has postponed the physical pain, the metaphysical pain. The most dramatic example of how Stevens recovers health in "Credences" comes with the foregrounding of "the old man standing on the tower" in canto III, the center of the poem's revisionary dialogue with "Esthétique du Mal":

> It is the old man standing on the tower,
> Who reads no book. His ruddy ancientness
> Absorbs the ruddy summer and is appeased,
> By an understanding that fulfills his age,
> By a feeling capable of nothing more.

This ancient reads no paragraphs on the sublime; he stands on his own rather than lie on his balcony at night. But the most remarkable difference becomes apparent when we juxtapose the old man with the soldier of time in "How red the rose that is the soldier's wound." Ruddiness replaces bloodiness, and appeasement comes within life rather than afterward. The old man can ripen into death, while the mountain upon which his Yeatsian tower stands is a natural mountain, not a shadowy hill composed of the restless dead.

So "Credences of Summer" can be read as an attempt to defuse the volcano. One aspect of this effort involves discovering a countersublime to take the place of catastrophe, something which commands awe but from which we do not shrink. Canto III provides just such an emblem in the totalizing vision of the all-encompassing "rock," domineering yet merciful:

> The rock cannot be broken. It is the truth.
> It rises from land and sea and covers them.
> It is a mountain half way green and then,
> The other immeasurable half, such rock
> As placid air becomes. But it is not
>
> A hermit's truth nor symbol in hermitage.
> It is the visible rock, the audible,
> The brilliant mercy of a sure repose,
> On this present ground, the vividest repose,
> Things certain sustaining us in certainty.

One might say that the rock opposes its audible mercy to the volcano's audible pain, its visible stability to the coming instability of the auroras. By claiming that "The rock cannot be broken. It is the truth," Stevens asserts his faith (soon to be challenged again) in our covenantal, or binding, relation to nature and to the truth. The apocalyptic mode of knowing involves the breaking apart of all merely temporal truths, including the planet of which we are part. But "Credences of Summer" also evolves a counterapocalypse in its evocation of a "trumpet of morning" whose blast, resounding over the divide of stanzas, unites rather than fractures:

> The resounding cry
> Is like ten thousand tumblers tumbling down
>
> To share the day.

To capture the essential difference between "The Auroras of Autumn" and "An Ordinary Evening in New Haven," we need only take the hint offered to us by Stevens in the name of the later poem's chief persona: Professor Eucalyptus. "Eucalyptus" means well covered, the very opposite of "apocalyptus" (to coin a word), and so if we call "Auroras" an apocalyptic poem, then the revision which follows it must be called eucalyptic. Unveiling the range of salutary meanings hidden in this term will be the purpose of my reading.

But perhaps the best way to begin to understand "Ordinary Evening" is to forget about hidden meanings and to invoke what lies on the surface, even though that region of the poem has also proved a little hard to see. For instance, critics seem not to have noticed the poem's overt religious imagery. "An Ordinary Evening in New Haven" is suffused with a sense of gratitude for a world returned:

It is fatal in the moon and empty there.
But, here, allons. The enigmatical
Beauty of each beautiful enigma

Becomes amassed in a total double-thing.
We do not know what is real and what is not.
We say of the moon, it is haunted by the man

Of bronze whose mind was made up and who, therefore, died.
We are not men of bronze and we are not dead.
His spirit is imprisoned in constant change.

But ours is not imprisoned. It resides
In a permanence composed of impermanence,
In a faithfulness as against the lunar light,

So that morning and evening are like promises kept,
So that the approaching sun and its arrival,
Its evening feast and the following festival,

This faithfulness of reality, this mode,
This tendance and venerable holding-in
Make gay the hallucinations in surfaces.

By banishing fatalism, Stevens banishes the serpent. The world is no longer perceived as his nest, but has been returned to us: hence, "allons." Later in "Ordinary Evening," Stevens will complicate this casting-out of the fatal by invoking the will of necessity, the "will of wills," but that is a much less malignant conception of fatalism than that found in the opening cantos of "Auroras." "An Ordinary Evening in New Haven" celebrates survival, and a line such as "We are not men of bronze and we are not dead" takes on great power when read against the fears of our extinction recorded in "Esthétique" and "Auroras." Words such as "permanence," "faithfulness," a phrase such as "It resides," record Stevens' conviction that we are here to stay, and so is our planet. After the threat of apocalypse, mere natural recurrence is no longer to be taken for granted, but is seen as a covenantal sign of "promises kept." The faintly Miltonic inversion of this phrase throws the weight where it should fall, on the solemn business of *keeping*. Also covenantal is the phrase "holding-in," which can be read as signifying almost precisely the opposite of apocalypse.

And yet, one finds little note of celebration in Stevens' well-known description of his intention in writing "Ordinary Evening": "here my intention is to try to get as close to the ordinary, the commonplace and ugly as it is possible for a poet to get. It is not a question of grim reality but of plain reality. The object of course is to purge oneself of anything false. . . . This is not in any sense a turning away from the ideas of 'Credences of Summer': it is a development of those ideas."[2] It is worth noting that the ugly is by no means synonymous with the ordinary or the commonplace; in fact, "Ordinary Evening" contains little ugliness, whether defined in terms of sight or sounds. The poem contains none of the intentional deformity Stevens occasionally brings to his language in order to express ugliness or violence. It may be that the process of "getting close" in and of itself is what Stevens means to celebrate, as he brings his poetry ever closer to its characteristic subjects. Yes, the world needs this new version, or translation, of its plain facts; but the translator also requires an intact text. The link Stevens draws between "Ordinary Evening" and "Credences of Summer" is interesting, for "Credences" offered nothing if not a plenary world, as well as a world momentarily at peace. We do not think of the world of "An Ordinary Evening in New Haven" as full in the same summery sense, and yet it is a capacious poem. "Ordinary Evening" is urban where "Credences" is pastoral, so its subject must also be what people have *made* of their world, for better or worse. Along with peace and the heroic return of the habitual—"War's miracle begetting that of peace," to quote "Mountains Covered with Cats"—comes the sorrow at what habit glosses over: namely, how deficient are our cultural forms of expression. But to counter this sense of "death's poverty"—a death-in-life—when it arises, the poem offers a redeeming figure, a holier version of Professor Eucalyptus. I refer to the Ecclesiast of canto XIX, "who chants in the dark / A text that is an answer, although obscure." Although late in the poem (canto XXVIII) Stevens seems to chastise himself for his failure to provide closure, the phrase "never-ending meditation" at the beginning signals to us that we are outside the sphere of sudden catastrophe, where death "may come tomorrow in the simplest word."

> The eye's plain version is a thing apart,
> The vulgate of experience. Of this,
> A few words, an and yet, and yet, and yet—
>
> As part of the never-ending meditation . . .

"An Ordinary Evening in New Haven" is not threatened by premature closure; it has a roominess to it, an ease. Its language is more transparent than that of the implosive "Auroras." As a never-ending meditation, "Ordinary Evening" never bids farewell to an idea, nor does it concern itself much with memory, for the poem searches out a "new resemblance of the sun." Though the vitality of the poem has been questioned, the first canto closes on a note of strength:

> As if the crude collops came together as one,
> A mythological form, a festival sphere,
> A great bosom, beard and being, alive with age.

By foreseeing a "larger audience" and a sage "alive with age," Stevens reverses the movement of both "Esthétique du Mal" and "Auroras," which had to work through their fears of apocalypse in order to find faith in survival. But we are alive from the beginning of "Ordinary Evening." And yet—to paraphrase the poem—"alive with age" gives critics room enough to demur, since they can always choose to stress the age or weariness of the speaker, rather than his vigor.

"An Ordinary Evening in New Haven" is a city

poem—an abstract one, to be sure—and while Stevens hardly celebrates New Haven, he does acknowledge its durability by according it the stubbornly honorific adjective of "difficult": "these houses, these difficult objects." The cities still stand, though Stevens goes on to say that they are "dilapidate," or a "hill of stones," as canto III puts it. It is as if Stevens were seeing the scene with double vision: beholding undeniable signs of endurance, while also marking a dilapidate scene, an aftermath of great destruction. This dilapidation may be a superimposition onto the scene in New Haven of all the destruction in the war, as if it were impossible to forget the fate of other cities, or to forgive the esthetic ruin of a city that escaped unscathed. The primary feeling, though, is the sense of sheer survival, since "The Auroras of Autumn" predicted that "the house will crumble and the books will burn." In the second canto, where Stevens supposes that the houses are mental constructs, he sees them illuminated in a fire of the mind, a "far-fire flowing," which should be set against the apocalyptic flames of "Auroras." "Ordinary Evening" celebrates the indestructibility of the poet's world, his never-ending meditation; better yet, it celebrates the return of space for the poet's characteristic obsessions. After "Esthétique" and "Auroras," who could have imagined that Stevens would ever find world enough and time to indulge

> In the perpetual reference, object
> Of the perpetual meditation, point
> Of the enduring, visionary love.

But let us not forget the site of "Ordinary Evening" as established in the third canto—"a hill of stones":

The point of vision and desire are the same.
It is to the hero of midnight that we pray
On a hill of stones to make beau mont thereof.

If it is misery that infuriates our love,
If the black of night stands glistening on beau mont,
Then, ancientest saint ablaze with ancientest truth,

Say next to holiness is the will thereto,
And next to love is the desire for love,
The desire for its celestial ease in the heart.

Which nothing can frustrate, that most secure,
Unlike love in possession of that which was
To be possessed and is. But this cannot

Possess. It is desire, set deep in the eye,
Behind all actual seeing, in the actual scene,
In the street, in a room, on a carpet or a wall,

Always in emptiness that would be filled,
In denial that cannot contain its blood,
A porcelain, as yet in the bats thereof.

An even darker reading, one that took the prophetic character of this poem into account, would see this hill as a type of the valley of bones. Stevens' prayer is not for resurrection but for transformation. He prays to the "hero of midnight," a new presence at that pole, supplanting the serpent from "Auroras":

These lights may finally attain a pole
In the midmost midnight and find the serpent there,

In another nest, the master of the maze . . .

No moment in "Ordinary Evening" better demonstrates the different aegis under which this poem of the aftermath is written. "Auroras" makes us feel that the end is near, "Ordinary Evening" that it has passed over, leaving us scarred but alive. Our new patron is a hero of midnight to whom we pray, not a serpent-master whom we deflect by capricious disobedience. In the figure of the "ancientest saint ablaze with ancientest truth"—a version of Yeats's sage in the holy fire[3]—Stevens elevates the hero of "Auroras," the scholar of one candle, into a pentecostal, living flame. "Auroras" ended with an image of "a blaze," but the saint, "ablaze," converts that destructiveness into a refining fire. He also seems to be a deliberate reworking of the rabbi, who was asked "to *read* . . . by these lights / Like a blaze of summer straw," while the saint is implored to "*Say* next to holiness is the will thereto."

Canto IV, a remarkable demonstration of what ought to be called Stevens' mode of implied social criticism, equates the dreariness of plainness with a kind of "savagery." "The plainness of plain things" is a trope for the grayness of civilized life—the other side of civil peace—a grayness Stevens equates with repressed savagery. Two types of poets are encountered in this canto. The first is one whose fight against illusion has resulted in the extinction of his genius:

> The plainness of plain things is savagery,
> As: the last plainness of a man who has fought
> Against illusion and was, in a great grinding
>
> Of growling teeth, and falls at night, snuffed out
> By the obese opiates of sleep.

The issue of plainness deepens as the canto goes on to describe how restless the people are in their peace, hungering as they do for genuine appeasement:

> Plain men in plain towns
> Are not precise about the appeasement they need.

They only know a savage assuagement cries
With a savage voice; and in that cry they hear
Themselves transposed, muted and comforted

In a savage and subtle and simple harmony,
A matching and mating of surprised accords,
A responding to a diviner opposite.

"Cry" is a crucial word in Stevens, most often standing for the untamable sound of nature, or human nature in agony. Although savage, this cry is recognizable, since it is both *vox clamantes* and *vox populi*. The cry emanates from a "diviner opposite," perhaps the Ecclesiast. It is certainly not the official voice of the "late president, Mr. Blank" (canto XXXI). The voice offers a prophetic cadence, "savage and subtle and simple," terms reminiscent of Milton's description of poetry as "simple, sensuous, and passionate."[4] The most subtle moment in Stevens' social psychology comes when he predicts that the people will hear themselves "muted" in that prophetic cry and that they will find that muting a comfort.

The cry reaches its apotheosis in the well-known twelfth canto, "The poem is the cry of its occasion, / Part of the res itself and not about it." Though graver meanings for "occasion" are certainly in order, it is still worth remembering that "Ordinary Evening," read before the Connecticut Academy of Arts and Sciences, was an occasional poem. (To its first auditors the poem, even in its eleven-canto format, must have seemed about as intelligible as a cry.) "Part of the res" can also be read as part of the "race," joining the poet to the collective (the "collops" of the opening canto) and reinforcing the proposition in "Men Made Out of Words" that "the whole race is a poet." There is a programmatic urgency to the canto, as exemplified in "There is no / Tomorrow for him," which makes it seem out of place within "Ordinary Evening" as a whole. If we treat this aberration as the eruption of a buried prophetic other, then the example of the Ecclesiast, who has sense enough not to chant into the wind, seems more cognate. The most remarkable thing about the canto is the way in which it seeks to return to the great, windy night of "Auroras," even though Stevens knows how difficult it is to face the wind: "What company, / In masks, can choir it with the naked wind?"

> The poet speaks the poem as it is,
>
> Not as it was: part of the reverberation
> Of a windy night as it is, when the marble statues
> Are like newspapers blown by the wind. He speaks
>
> By sight and insight as they are. There is no
> Tomorrow for him. The wind will have passed by,
> The statues will have gone back to be things about.

This particular canto displays a rare nostalgia in Stevens for the apocalyptic or violent moment. But Stevens has never been the sort of singer who could trumpet it with the wind. In "Domination of Black," the great example of a "turning in the wind," the poet confessed: "I felt afraid." Indeed, to be "part of the reverberation of a windy night as it is" means being echoic rather than immediate. "Ordinary Evening" dwells in the aftermath, or the reverberation, of "Auroras." The wind *has* already passed by. The people have gone back to getting their news from the newspapers, rather than from the ominous wind blowing through them and their land. The following canto, acknowledging this, records the poet's protest: "He skips the journalism of subjects."

The eucalyptic program of "Ordinary Evening" is spelled out quite beautifully in canto XXII, the second of the Professor's cantos and the only one to appear in the original version of the poem:

> Professor Eucalyptus said, "The search
> For reality is as momentous as
> The search for god." It is the philosopher's search
>
> For an interior made exterior
> And the poet's search for the same exterior made
> Interior: breathless things broodingly abreath
>
> With the inhalations of original cold
> And of original earliness. Yet the sense
> Of cold and earliness is a daily sense,
>
> Not the predicate of bright origin.
> Creation is not renewed by images
> Of lone wanderers. To re-create, to use
>
> The cold and earliness and bright origin
> Is to search. Likewise to say of the evening star,
> The most ancient light in the most ancient sky,
>
> That it is wholly an inner light, that it shines
> From the sleepy bosom of the real, re-creates,
> Searches a possible for its possibleness.

What Stevens says here about the search for reality is less important than his denial of the need to return to origins in order to recapture the "sense / Of cold and earliness." At the end of "The Idea of Order at Key West," Stevens drove a wedge between "ourselves and . . . our origins," fearing as he did "the grinding water and the gasping wind," the sea of origins. Now he would substitute a "daily sense" for the ruinous quest of the "lone wanderer." Since the quotidian is usually regarded as the opposite of the original, this is a daring substitution. But such a move keeps faith with the spirit of "Ordinary Evening," which aims to save the appearances. The turn from origins to ends in the canto comes about because Stevens has linked the two through their relation to apocalyptic knowledge, which can apply to the beginning as well as the end of things. For a poet, the end proper is encompassed in the image of the evening star, lodestar of poetic immortality. By internalizing that light, declaring it to be "wholly an inner light" (a holy inner light), Stevens would thereby "stellify" himself, place himself within the constellation of tradition by removing that constellation to his own bosom. Better yet, Stevens would find the sign of election within himself, rather than await formal canonization by the tradition. Stevens abhors the idea of being a poetic star "in lone splendor hung aloft," to quote the Keatsian paradigm;[5] thus the process of internalization represents the ideal of a living tradition in which re-creation becomes a daily sense, and the firmament of great poets is found within us. The "possible" that Stevens searches for "its possibleness" may be a paradigm of poetic immortality that he can live with.

The stars are much on Stevens' mind in this period. In "Auroras" they are seen as warriors within the context of Armageddon, where the whole idea of tradition is threatened by extinction. Needless to say, the light of such stars cannot be internalized. In "Large Red Man Reading," a lyric written between "Auroras" and "Ordinary Evening," Stevens takes revenge against the domineering set of the stars by imagining their inhabitants, the dead poets, mourning their lost place on earth. Here Stevens goes even beyond the satire on the metaphysicals in the last canto of "Esthétique du Mal":

There were ghosts that returned to earth to hear his
  phrases,
As he sat there reading, aloud, the great blue tabulae.
They were those from the wilderness of stars that had
  expected more.

There were those that returned to hear him read from
  the poem of life,
Of the pans above the stove, the pots on the table, the
  tulips among them.
They were those that would have wept to step barefoot
  into reality,

That would have wept and been happy, have shivered in
  the frost
And cried out to feel it again, have run fingers over leaves
And against the most coiled thorn, have seized on what
  was ugly

And laughed, as he sat there reading, from out of the
  purple tabulae,
The outlines of being and its expressings, the syllables of
  its law:
Poesis, poesis, the literal characters, the vatic lines,

Which in those ears and in those thin, those spended
  hearts,
Took on color, took on shape and the size of things as
  they are
And spoke the feeling for them, which was what they
  had lacked.

The ghosts who wish to step barefoot into reality must do so through the mediating phrases of the "Large Red Man Reading" (Stevens' birthplace was

Reading, Pa.). Milton entered Blake's left foot; these ghosts enter the living poet via "the sleepy bosom of reality." The poem illustrates the descendental theme with a vengeance, shifting the locus of power from on high to below. In this regard, it is worth comparing "Large Red Man Reading" to a poem of thirty years earlier, "Nuances of a Theme by Williams," where the evening star is celebrated for its lonely hauteur:

> Shine alone, shine nakedly, shine like bronze,
> that reflects neither my face nor any inner part
> of my being, shine like fire, that mirrors nothing.

"Large Red Man Reading" recoils from the traditional association of the stars with the immortal substances of art. Expressing weariness with the rigors of immortality, the later poem has the ghosts exchange fire for frost, bronze for pots and pans.

I have been arguing that "Ordinary Evening" is a poem of healing or recovery, a poem of gradual ascents and veiled cognitions. Stevens avoids, or is avoided by, catastrophic recognitions in the poem; this extends to the recognition of the poet's deep origins in "The mother's face / The purpose of the poem." The muse figure Stevens does encounter in "Ordinary Evening" is much more of a fraternal presence. To see the muse-mother unveiled is to see the face of death, but the masculine watcher (whose eyes alone are visible) is associated with life:

> Life fixed him, wandering on the stair of glass,
> With its attentive eyes. And, as he stood,
> On his balcony, outsensing distances,
>
> There were looks that caught him out of empty air.
> *C'est toujours la vie qui me regarde* . . . This was
> Who watched him, always, for unfaithful thought.

This sat beside his bed, with its guitar,
To keep him from forgetting, without a word,
A note or two disclosing who it was.

Nothing about him ever stayed the same,
Except his hidalgo and his eye and tune,
The shawl across one shoulder and the hat.

The commonplace became a rumpling of blazons.
What was real turned into something most unreal,
Bare beggar-tree, hung low for fruited red

In isolated moments—isolations
Were false. The hidalgo was permanent, abstract,
A hatching that stared and demanded an answering look.

"Life fixed him": Stevens clearly intends this restorative fastening of the eye to be compared to the eyes which "open and fix on us in every sky." No terror attends the sense of being watched here. The French sentence links the hidalgo to the hidden self brought to the surface with the aid of French in "Sea Surface Full of Clouds": *mon frère, mon esprit bâtard,* etc. The intimacy between poet and hidalgo is further conveyed by the pun in "his eye and tune": his "I and tu," or "I and thou." The hidalgo measures Stevens' faithfulness to life, now that the poem has established the faithfulness of reality. And by way of a sign, the hidalgo causes the "bare limbs, bare trees" of "Auroras" to be hung not with the ghastly fruit of the dead poet and his beloved, but with "fruited red." Under his dispensation, the dead tree comes to life.

No long poem of Stevens' makes so much issue of starting and stopping as "Ordinary Evening." As J. Hillis Miller puts it: "It is a supple and sinuous improvisation, constantly generating itself out of its own annihilation."[6] "Annihilation" violates the mood of the poem, I would argue, but "generating itself" is exactly the way to describe the poem's perpetual sense of fecundity. In fact, Miller's phrase serves as a perfect gloss on the canto in which the theme of beginning and ending is linked specifically to generation:

> Reality is the beginning not the end,
> Naked Alpha, not the hierophant Omega,
> Of dense investiture, with luminous vassals.
>
> It is the infant A standing on infant legs,
> Not twisted, stooping, polymathic Z,
> He that kneels always on the edge of space
>
> In the pallid perceptions of its distances.
> Alpha fears men or else Omega's men
> Or else his prolongations of the human.
>
> These characters are around us in the scene.
> For one it is enough; for one it is not;
> For neither is it profound absentia,
>
> Since both alike appoint themselves the choice
> Custodians of the glory of the scene,
> The immaculate interpreters of life.
>
> But that's the difference: in the end and the way
> To the end. Alpha continues to begin.
> Omega is refreshed at every end.

As Omega reaches his end, he seems to generate his own offspring, Alpha. Omega's prolongations of the human include his parental extension of self. The sudden generation or appearance of a redemptive child is an image we will find in a number of late Stevens poems, but nowhere else does it come about so smoothly. Of course, the infant A is contained within the alphabetical system whose end is already known, and so this particular child can bring no apocalyptic knowledge of the new. The late poem "A Discovery of Thought" presents another sort of child, "an antipodal, far-fetched creature," who brings "an immaculate disclosure of the secret no more obscured."[7]

The gliding measure of "Ordinary Evening" formalizes its thematic principle of noncatastrophic endings. The poem comes to seem like an incessant device, or homemade machine, for the production of verses. How *would* such a poem be brought to closure? As all students of Stevens know, the question gave the poet some trouble. Perhaps we make too much of the fact that the original eleven-canto version ended with canto XXIX; after all, Stevens read the first version aloud, and he might have judged that a fabular ending would prove more dramatic, if not necessarily clearer. And yet there is something about Stevens' juggling of endings that seems paradigmatic in this case, as if a poem such as this almost demanded the possibility of multiple endings. In any event, the final four cantos of the long version were always its final four, and as a group they create a sense of coming upon a variously defined end. Canto XXVIII, the least problematic of the four, introduces the triad of endings by announcing that "Ordinary Evening" is an "endlessly elaborating poem." From this point on, much nimbleness is required of the interpreter in order to sort out what is at stake in the proposed conclusions.

Canto XXIX, now the antepenultimate section, flatters the titular locale of "Ordinary Evening" by working elm trees into its parable. (New Haven is known as the Elm City, though the elms are no more, having been destroyed by a change of nature, namely the elm blight of the 1950s.) The canto builds to a single-line, epitaphic summary of the wandering mariners' career: "Their dark-colored words had redescribed the citrons." Does Stevens intend this as a statement of strength or limitation? The mariners seem to have reached the end of their quest, since Stevens tells us that they "came to the land of the lemon trees, / At last . . ." This lemony land conforms to the mythological locus Stevens called the visionary south, an island that lies even beyond the ken of the Floridian vision. But when the mariners arrive in this land they insist, rather perversely, that they are simply back in their last port of call: "They said, 'We are back once more in the land of the elm trees, / But folded over, turned round.'"

Jokes are being played throughout this canto, though on whom and by whom are not quite clear. By folding over and turning around *e-l-m*, one gets close enough to *l-e-m-o-n* to see one reason why the mariners claim that the countries are reversible. But the real question centers on whether the mariners' illusion, their form of double vision, results in an addition to nature or merely a blindness to place. Are the mariners changing the land by describing it well or only importing their idiosyncrasy? When the mariners insist on the similarity between lemon and elm countries, they are really insisting on the likeness between the earthly paradise and our native climate that Stevens always maintained. Even as they arrive in the greater Florida they bid farewell to it, if only by retaining "their dark-colored words." So the poem journeys between opposites. To appreciate how true this is, we must catch the joke at the beginning of the canto, where the "narrator," *not* the mariners, also folds language over, turns it around:

In the land of the lemon trees, yellow and yellow were
Yellow-blue, yellow-green, pungent with citron-sap,
Dangling and spangling, the mic-mac of mocking birds.

In the land of the elm trees, wandering mariners
Looked on big women, whose ruddy-ripe images
Wreathed round and round the round wreath of autumn.

They rolled their r's, there, in the land of the citrons.
In the land of big mariners, the words they spoke
Were mere brown clods, mere catching weeds of talk.

The inhabitants may roll their *r*'s in the land of the citrons, but the narrator certainly does not. He describes the lemon trees in a northern tongue: "Dangling and spangling . . ." Conversely, the land of the elm trees in the second tercet is all rolling *r*'s. With this narrator as guide, it is no wonder the mariners have difficulty knowing where they are. Metaphorical language is always wandering, guided by the lodestar of the duly opposite: so the mariners and the narrator behold a southerly north, a northerly south. Stevens tempers the triumph of this technique by leaving open the possibility that the mariners are, after all, only deluded, incapable of seeing what is truly there. The deepest question to be wrung from this parable may be: have the restless mariners earned the pleasures of the visionary south by refusing to recognize them, or lost them for that same reason?

The legacy of canto XXIX, however questionably established, has to do with our capacity to alter nature through language and thereby become "part of what it is." In canto XXX, the parable of legacy goes underground and what emerges is a description that seems anything but redescribed. The landscape presented appears without human trace; even our houses are gone, replaced by the tree-caves of squirrels:

> The last leaf that is going to fall has fallen.
> The robins are là-bas, the squirrels, in tree-caves,
> Huddle together in the knowledge of squirrels.
>
> The wind has blown the silence of summer away.
> It buzzes beyond the horizon or in the ground:
> In mud under ponds, where the sky used to be reflected.
>
> The barrenness that appears is an exposing.
> It is not part of what is absent, a halt
> For farewells, a sad hanging on for remembrances.
>
> It is a coming on and a coming forth.
> The pines that were fans and fragrances emerge,
> Staked solidly in a gusty grappling with rocks.
>
> The glass of the air becomes an element—
> It was something imagined that has been washed away.
> A clearness has returned. It stands restored.
>
> It is not an empty clearness, a bottomless sight.
> It is a visibility of thought,
> In which hundreds of eyes, in one mind, see at once.

No canto more starkly illustrates how "Ordinary Evening" inhabits the zone of *afterwards*, the zone of survival. And yet, what seems to have survived here is what Vendler terms "the human substitute":[8] the squirrels, for example, standing in for the family huddled in the shelter of "Auroras." What has happened to the resolute commonplace of New Haven? The answer is that in these final cantos, Stevens detaches himself from the world of the poem, much as he does at the end of "Credences of Summer." Indeed, he begins to plot the strategy of his detachment from the world. The disappearance of the human from canto xxx is a prefiguration of the poet's own withdrawal. More crucially, this canto tries to foresee the shape of his survival after death. It is as if, having borne witness to the continued existence of ordinary reality after the shock of threatened apocalypse, Stevens was turning here to the question of his own continuation.

The poem this question engenders is perhaps the most vigorous and, necessarily, the most circuitous in "Ordinary Evening." Its vigor is unmistakable, as Stevens harnesses the power of cold by imagining winter in terms of birth and resurrection: a coming forth, an emergence. This canto should be set alongside the second section of "Auroras," where cold and blankness threaten to obliterate the poet. But here Stevens has journeyed beyond obliteration. "The barrenness that appears is an exposing," not an effacing. At this moment, Stevens stakes a claim to winter as the ground of his continuing identity. This immanent mode of survival exists alongside the startling gesture of exaltation which arises at the end of the canto, that uncanny image of "hundreds of eyes, in one mind." Stevens is doing nothing less than substituting those eyes—which must be "his"—for the stars. He is also, of course, revising (in the literal sense) the opening tercet of "Auroras." Gone is the paranoia associated with a serpent "whose head is air"; after all, this "is not an empty clearness, a bottomless sight. / It is a visibility of thought." One is tempted to say that Stevens gives back to the skies the star that he had internalized in canto XXII, except that these stars, or starry thoughts, shine out of one mind. Instead of being watched, Stevens does the watching, assuming the high prerogative of the departed poet. Instead of internalizing the evening star, he internalizes the whole of the night and then projects the stars into "outer" space. In "A Rabbit as King of the Ghosts," written in 1936, Stevens created a phantasmagoric creature who kept growing larger and larger:

> You are humped higher and higher, black as stone,
> You sit with your head like a carving in space . . .

And "Credences of Summer" ended with an image of the creator at play in the sky meadows of the mind. Earlier in canto xxx, Stevens bade the robins adieu—"the robins are là-bas"—and with them, the Keatsian route of escape. For there is no desire in him to escape this place; rather, Stevens becomes its daemonic overseer. As Whitman in "Crossing Brooklyn Ferry," so Stevens:

> Who knows, for all the distance, but I am as good as
> looking at you, for all you cannot see me?

The canto Stevens settled on for his finale descends from the stars to vaunt the eye's microscopic (perhaps X-ray-like) power to see through "outer shields," paring away grosser versions of reality in order to arrive at the imagination's "finikin" forms. Though Stevens refers to "final form" (finikin's wake?), the string of appositives suggests that finality may be postponed indefinitely in the interests of the never-ending meditation:

> The less legible meanings of sounds, the little reds
> Not often realized, the lighter words
> In the heavy drum of speech, the inner men
>
> Behind the outer shields, the sheets of music
> In the strokes of thunder, dead candles at the window
> When day comes, fire-foams in the motions of the sea,

Flickings from finikin to fine finikin
And the general fidget from busts of Constantine
To photographs of the late president, Mr. Blank,

These are the edgings and inchings of final form,
The swarming activities of the formulae
Of statement, directly and indirectly getting at,

Like an evening evoking the spectrum of violet,
A philosopher practicing scales on his piano,
A woman writing a note and tearing it up.

Even if the scholar of one candle does not live to see the morning, there will be "a new scholar replacing an older one," to quote "Looking across the Fields and Watching the Birds Fly," an even later poem, as the race keeps fidgeting to adjust itself to its surroundings. The closing tercet of "Ordinary Evening" has an epitaphic starkness even though it undercuts the very notion of solidity:

> It is not in the premise that reality
> Is a solid. It may be a shade that traverses
> A dust, a force that traverses a shade.

These lines epitomize the closing gesture so often favored by Stevens: a descent, or a reduction, to power. Despite the thoroughness of his whittling (and he seems to anticipate the reductions of subatomic physics), Stevens discovers that life is ineradicable, so long as the action of "traversing," the crossing of planes, can take place. When a shade traverses a dust, or a force traverses a shade, basic principles of life are set in motion: "And the spirit of God moved upon the face of the waters." By pursuing the shade of creative force down this far, Stevens shows that it can survive even the shattering of the solid world, not to mention the loss of "these houses, these difficult objects." From the insubstantial trinity of force, dust, and shade, a swarm of new activity will always emerge.

4

The Mythology of Modern Death: "The Owl in the Sarcophagus" and "To an Old Philosopher in Rome"

Stevens wrote so frequently in the elegiac mode, and drew such strength from it, that any attempt to isolate pure elegy in his poetry would be pointless. A sophisticated anatomy of his work would produce innumerable forms of farewell: for, like his alphabetical persona Omega, Stevens seems always to have been "refreshed at every end." If we glance back to the earlier poetry, perhaps the most interesting elegiac expressions can be found in those poems which associate death with poetic failure: "The Comedian as the Letter C," "Anglais Mort à Florence," "Landscape with Boat." These poems serve Stevens as a means of exorcising dangerous tendencies within himself; by tracing the decline of a substitutive persona, Stevens manages to save himself for poetry. But the predominant form of elegy in the earlier Stevens is captured in spare, epitaphic poems such as "The Death of a Soldier," which evoke the ghostliest of figures. Accustomed as we are to think of Stevens as a poet of earth, it still ought to surprise us when we realize how thoroughly he has excised the eschatological dimension from the elegy. If traditional elegies can be said to enter "the enlarged space that the dead apparently create for the living,"[1] however fearful that space, then Stevens can be said to avoid speculation upon such terra incognita, as well as the formal or traditional apparatus of the elegy which transports us there.

"The Owl in the Sarcophagus" (1947) is the obvious exception in the Stevens canon, although I will argue in my next chapter that the brief lyrics composed at the very end of Stevens' career, the cluster of poems following "The Rock," should also be read as meditations upon the shape of the poet's survival. But "Owl" is the most overt poem of discovery in the Stevens canon, rivaled only by "Auroras," written a few months afterward. "To an Old Philosopher in Rome," composed five years after "The Owl in the Sarcophagus," is the only other poem by Stevens which might be read as a formal elegy, although, in complex ways which I will explore, it works to revise the prophetic or visionary mode of elegy advanced in the earlier poem.

"The Owl in the Sarcophagus" has been called "the least accessible of Stevens' major poems,"[2] and it has certainly drawn the fewest readings. The complexity of its imagery is daunting even by its author's standards, and the density of internal reference to other Stevens poems, generally an aid to interpretation, seems to be kept deliberately low. The poem might also be regarded as the least assimilable of Stevens' long poems, for its speculations on the end of imagination are not of the sort that easily generate other poems. They remain fixed in the mind, visionary prodigies rather than paradigms.

The occasion for the elegy was the death of Stevens' closest friend, Henry Church. It is axiomatic that great elegies concern the poet's own fate more than that of the deceased, whether the latter is a rival poet or hero. I would suppose that the most salient fact to keep in mind about Henry Church is that he was a patron of the arts and that he and Stevens had intended to establish what they called a Poetry Chair.[3] This investment in the institution of poetry is worth considering in the context of what "Owl" reveals about what might be termed the afterlife of imagination. For if the poem avoids the relentless self-allusiveness of other major poems of Stevens, it compensates by gathering up the whole of elegiac tradition in the great image of the winding-sheet, a flowing robe or tapestry of the imagination. Harold Bloom has centered the ancestry of "Owl" in "The Sleepers" and "When Lilacs Last in the Dooryard Bloomed," especially in the latter's triadic configuration of the poet and the two figures Whitman calls "the knowledge of death" and "the thought of death."[4] For the genesis of Stevens' three forms that move about the night, one might also point to a lesser poem, Keats's "Ode on Indolence," where we encounter a linked ensemble of "Poesy," "Love," and "Ambition." That last figure interests me the most in terms of "Owl," for it bears most closely upon the elegiac poet's inevitable placement of himself within tradition. And, as my reading will demonstrate, Yeats once again hovers over the scene, as he tends to when Stevens is writing in the sublime mode.

A last word, however, on the question of elegiac

tradition before turning to a reading of "The Owl in the Sarcophagus." Bloom points to Stevens' repression of Whitman as a source of the poem's power,[5] but the extent of Stevens' deliberate forgetting or eliding of primordial elegiac metaphors might go even deeper. For Whitman, the assassination of Lincoln in the early spring was a solemn coincidence verifying the elegiac poet's seasonal trope of death and rebirth. The severity of internalization in "Owl" can best be seen in the avoidance of any reference to spring in the poem: for not only did Henry Church die in the early spring but, as it happens, he died on Good Friday.[6] Perhaps the depth of Stevens' feeling for Church and for his vision can best be measured by the excision of any occasional detail from the poem, even when those accidents might validate the enduring tropes of poetic mourning and consolation. It is as if "The Owl in the Sarcophagus" discovers a haunt of prophecy that endures beyond April's green.

> Two forms move among the dead, high sleep
> Who by his highness quiets them, high peace
> Upon whose shoulders even the heavens rest,
>
> Two brothers. And a third form, she that says
> Good-by in the darkness, speaking quietly there,
> To those that cannot say good-by themselves.
>
> These forms are visible to the eye that needs,
> Needs out of the whole necessity of sight.
> The third form speaks, because the ear repeats,
>
> Without a voice, inventions of farewell.
> These forms are not abortive figures, rocks,
> Impenetrable symbols, motionless. They move
>
> About the night. They live without our light,
> In an element not the heaviness of time,
> In which reality is prodigy.

The most intriguing of these figures is certainly the third form, the woman. She is situated between life and death, but enjambment nudges her toward death's side, for the utterance can be read: "And *death* cries quickly." She is past life, but not yet into death; this is a region Stevens will come to explore increasingly in the last poems. In "Of Mere Being," for example, it becomes the space between the last thought and the end of the mind.

The odd thing about this cry is that the woman almost seems to be the dying one: "I am gone." She beseeches the departing ones—"those that cannot say good-by themselves"—to remain true to her memory of them:

> Keep you, keep you, I am gone, oh keep you as
> My memory.

This is intensely interesting and difficult. Are we meant to supply "of you" in brackets after the last two words: "My memory [of you]"? In other words, are the dead being implored to remain true to the earth-mother's memory of them as they were? In this reading, the mother would be the source of memory. But it also seems possible to regard the phrase as meaning that the dead *are* "My memory"; the dead embody the memory of the world. The dead *remember* where they came from, and that memory somehow keeps the world alive. Dead poets especially are keepers of the world's memory, are kept alive insofar as they keep memory alive. "Keep you" is an archaism and also an irrational or onomatopoetic construction, resembling a bird's cheeping. (Compare the bird's "scrawny cry" in "Not Ideas about the Thing but the Thing Itself.") The phrase can be brooded upon until its stable meaning, if it has any, is dissolved; surely Stevens intended this for the cry between life and death. On any level, however, the phrase does read like an exhortation to faithfulness. Whether the mother does the work of memory, or the dead do the keeping, this is the earth's voice crying out, not the voice of the dead. "Keep you, keep you," can easily glide into the contrary: keep me, keep me. In any case, *keeping* may be viewed as the prime labor of poetic elegy, if not of poetry itself.[7]

The second canto might have opened the poem, since it presents an image of the poetic quester setting out on his journey:

> There came a day, there was a day—one day
> A man walked living among the forms of thought
> To see their lustre truly as it is . . .

Stevens seems to be stuttering over the phrasing of this dark day, perhaps the day of Henry Church's death, as he approximates the elegist's traditional trouble in beginning his lament. "Among the dead," from the last canto, has now become "among the forms of thought," the underworld in which the structure of things at last reveals itself. It has been suggested that "A man walked living" refers to Church,[8] but surely it is the poet himself who goes to the underworld in order to "Follow after, O my companion, my fellow, my self." The four stanzas of this canto provide a lyric abstract of the motives for the descent in the great epics—those instances of "abysmal melody"—and do so in phrases which are almost all Stevensian key signatures at this point in his career:

And in harmonious prodigy to be,
A while, conceiving his passage as into a time
That of itself stood still, perennial,

Less time than place, less place than thought of place
And, if of substance, a likeness of the earth,
That by resemblance twanged him through and through,

Releasing an abysmal melody,
A meeting, an emerging in the light,
A dazzle of remembrance and of sight.

The first four words of canto III—"There he saw well"—capture the visionary clarity attained on this journey. "There" is the peculiar marker of the visionary realm, while "saw" conveys a privileged or prophetic mode of seeing which Stevens gives uncanny emphasis to by adding "well." "There he saw well" corrects the limitations of earthly sight; Yeats's line from "The Wild Swans at Coole," "I saw before I had well finished," may be in Stevens' mind at this point, providing an example of partial vision.

But what exactly does Stevens see, what is the content of his vision? Despite the promise of revelation, the poet seems to see coverings rather than uncoverings:

> There he saw well the foldings in the height
> Of sleep, the whiteness folded into less,
> Like many robings . . .

Even at this height, things are still hidden for the "living" man who walks among the dead. The living man either sees the folds which will be unfolded upon death—and which Henry Church, the subject of the elegy, sees now—or sees that the truth will always remain folded, the book remain closed. If "foldings" are taken to mean seals, then it would require a greater apocalypse than that of mere death to open the Book. Stevens, as epic follower in the land of the dead, sees what can be seen upon death, which is to say that he sees the folds that require unfolding. Considering the nature of Stevens' temperament, such an unfolding will probably reveal only further coverings. As a living man, furthermore, Stevens situates himself on the near side of the vanishing point, the outer side of the gold. Indeed, if we see the fold as a shroud—Yeats's "Cuchulain Comforted" comes to mind—it is clear why Stevens remains on the outer side of "the whiteness folded into less." Following after, Stevens discovers that the dead are in motion, perhaps moving away from him:

> As a moving mountain is, moving through day
> And night, colored from distances, central
> Where luminous agitations come to rest,
>
> In an ever-changing, calmest unity,
> The unique composure, harshest streakings joined
> In a vanishing-vanished violet that wraps round
>
> The giant body the meanings of its folds,
> The weaving and the crinkling and the vex,
> As on water of an afternoon in the wind
>
> After the wind has passed.

The vision here seems closer to that of the mountainous body of all the dead in "Esthétique du Mal," canto VII. The bodies of the dead become "the giant body," as Stevens substitutes the figure of the mountain for the traditional pile of fallen leaves.

Canto III closes with a true flight "beyond the fire." After describing what he sees in terms of folds, wrinklings, and vexed robings, Stevens focuses on the blazing "whiteness that is the ultimate intellect."

> Sleep realized
> Was the whiteness that is the ultimate intellect,
> A diamond jubilance beyond the fire,
>
> That gives its power to the wild-ringed eye.
> Then he breathed deeply the deep atmosphere
> Of sleep, the accomplished, the fulfilling air.

It is impossible to tell who has experienced "sleep realized," but it seems most likely that the quester in the land of the dead is casting his "wild-ringed eye" upon a surmise of what the dead themselves must know; he himself cannot pass beyond the fire, but he imagines the realm of ultimate intellect. Stevens can only approach this region, although he comes close enough to breathe in its atmosphere. "Breath" and "breathing" are strong terms in Stevens, almost always used to signify the poetic faculty and the climate in which it thrives. That climate is usually naturalistic; to breathe deeply means to inhale the essence of life on earth, as in "Notes" (*"It Must Change"*):

> Tonight the lilacs magnify
> The easy passion, the ever-ready love
> Of the lover that lies within us and we breathe
>
> An odor evoking nothing, absolute.
> We encounter in the dead middle of the night
> The purple odor, the abundant bloom.
>
> The lover sighs as for accessible bliss,
> Which he can take within him on his breath.

"The Owl in the Sarcophagus" shows Stevens breathing in the atmosphere of the beyond, and though he must return to earth, his sense of what air nourishes the deepest inhalation has been changed.

The central figure in the poem's triad is also its most puzzling. In a poem as mystery-laden as "The Owl in the Sarcophagus" it is redundant to talk of puzzles, but the fourth canto presents tonal, if not verbal, complexities, surpassing those of any other canto. The lines on peace, or "peace after death," are disturbing as well as enigmatic, since more than a touch of the sinister creeps into the representation of this centaurlike guardian, "the godolphin and fellow."

> There peace, the godolphin and fellow, estranged,
> estranged,
> Hewn in their middle as the beam of leaves,
> The prince of shither-shade and tinsel lights,
>
> Stood flourishing the world. The brilliant height
> And hollow of him by its brillance calmed,
> Its brightness burned the way good solace seethes.

In the epigraph to "Notes toward a Supreme Fiction," Stevens characterized peace as a "vivid transparence." Here it is anything but transparent. As the figure of peace flickers across Stevens' sight it will assume a number of phantasmagoric shapes, but none more difficult to decipher than this opening one. A godolphin is an Arabian stallion, a "godolphin and fellow," presumably, a horse and rider, or equestrian statue. (Just as one should not overlook the presence of god in godolphin, so "dolphin" should not be ignored, with its Yeatsian resonance. I will soon show what the state of peace-after-death has in common with Yeats's "Byzantium.") Statues fill Stevens' poems where generally they are regarded as premature ideas of order, states of peace achieved at the cost of living change. Most memorably, from "Notes," there is the mounted General Du Puy, cast in "the nerveless frame / Of a suspension, a permanence, so rigid / That it made the General a bit absurd." Peace seems to be both horse *and* rider, animal and human, a condition Stevens sees as estranged—as if peace, oddly enough, were not at peace with itself. This would be in accord with the dictum that "the imperfect is our paradise," and yet such a note of division does not appear comforting. But there is little about peace that soothes—indeed, the peace that he brings *seethes*. Stevens chooses to see him in these opening tercets as something of a poseur, another of those suspicious sleight-of-hand men. Does the elegy, then, move to uncover a falsehood in our conception of peace?

Perhaps the question can best be approached by hearkening to Stevens' recognition of the figure before him as "peace after death." "The Owl in the Sarcophagus" proceeds in a region where all the tropes come true, but in the case of peace such truth borders dangerously upon falsehood. No longer is peace the aim of a summer prayer, as in "The House Was Quiet and the World Was Calm," or "Credences of Summer." Nor is Stevens leaving peace unimaged as Eliot does at the end of "The Waste Land," where "Shantih, Shantih, Shantih" invokes the peace that passes understanding. Peace has been attained, but at the price of death. Such a price demands scrutiny of the reward to which the subject of the elegy has gone and where the poet will soon follow. Rewards have to do with ends, and Stevens is now beholding not only an end to an imaginative man, Henry Church, but the end of the imagination as well. For in the preceding canto, Stevens-as-quester seemed to be exerting his power of visionary sight even as he observed the bourne of "sleep realized." He remained still within the circle of the wild-ringed eye; his ability to breathe deeply indicated that the poetic spirit was suspiring, not expiring. In fact, the canto on sleep seems to have nothing to do with the notion of death. Moving into the realm of peace, however, changes everything. Peace is an end state, the place where the imagination finally comes to rest. Another way of describing the difference between the cantos centers on the distinction between the "ultimate intellect" of canto III and "generations of the imagination" in canto IV. The former, a condition of sleep, posits a continuity between earthly faculties and what is left to us "beyond the fire," even if the material foundations of intellect are shed. But, as the hieratic robe swathing peace makes clear, the imagination is literally wrapped up in its material. This dialectical distinction between imaged and unimaged intellect lies at the very heart of Stevens' last poetry.

Stevens sees peace as being clothed in a ceremonial robe or shroud. Unlike the shrouds sewn by the shades in Yeats's "Cuchulain Comforted," this robe is composed of the "fictive weavings" (to quote the character of Ozymandias in "Notes") spun by the living—in other words, their poems.

> Generations of the imagination piled
> In the manner of its stitchings, of its thread,
> In the weaving round the wonder of its need,
>
> And the first flowers upon it, an alphabet
> By which to spell out holy doom and end,
> A bee for the remembering of happiness.
>
> Peace stood with our last blood adorned, last mind,
> Damasked in the originals of green,
> A thousand begettings of the broken bold.

Stevens never achieved a more totalizing vision than this extraordinary glimpsing of the whole body of imagination. Its only rival would be his sighting of the mother's face in "Auroras." The temporal generations are laid out in spatial simultaneity upon this grand tapestry (really a tapestry-within-a-tapestry, since the figures who parade through the poem are also woven around the urnlike sarcophagus). The sight of the "generations . . . piled" is one we associate with the epic quester's vision of all the dead heaped on the shore: "I had not thought death had undone so many." And the products of imagination do seem to strike Stevens as more than a little deathly, as if all the sheets of composition, in the end, came down to winding-sheets. The alphabet ("A bee"), the flowers, are items in a Book of the Dead, with peace its mummified priest. The corner of this particular mausoleum is hardly a poet's paradise. However resplendent its flowing robe of texts, peace guards over a dead tradition, tradition regarded as the equivalent of death.

As I mentioned in regard to the word "godolphin" and the possible puns it contains, "The Owl in the Sarcophagus" engages the Yeats of "Byzantium," but Stevens draws close only to reinforce the distance between the two. "A thousand begettings of the broken bold" summons Yeats most overtly, highlighting as it does the crucial verbs "break" and "beget" in the final stanza of "Byzantium":

> Astraddle on the dolphin's mire and blood,
> Spirit after spirit:
>
> The golden smithies of the Emperor!
> Marbles of the dancing floor
> Break bitter furies of complexity,

Those images that yet
Fresh images beget,
That dolphin-torn, that gong-tormented sea.

Most commentators agree that Yeats is standing in Byzantium and looking outward—sub specie aeternitatis—as the living are converted into the dead. How much he rejoices at this vision, where his sympathies lie, is at question: the stanza splits power both ways, between the force of "break" (belonging to the artisans of eternity) and that of "beget" (belonging to the fecundity of the living). Stevens' "Peace after death" is more of a weaver than a smithy, but he also converts living material into eternal forms. Stevens, however, shows considerably less ambivalence than Yeats when it comes to the value of earthly begettings, and his sense of the "broken," though less overtly violent than Yeats's, contains more elegiac pathos. Stevens' fervor is displayed in the choice of "bold" as a trope for the poet, a revelation of his heroism in the aftermath of ruin.

The conclusion to this unsettling canto hypostatizes "peace after death" in terms that are all wrong for Stevens:

This is that figure stationed at our end,
Always, in brilliance, fatal, final, formed
Out of our lives to keep us in our death,

To watch us in the summer of Cyclops
Underground, a king as candle by our beds
In a robe that is our glory as he guards.

By wrong, I mean intolerable. This Statue at the World's End[9] appropriates all glory to himself, in a robe that is a rob, since it is our glory. As will also be true in "Of Mere Being,"[10] we are left uncertain as to who has stationed this figure, who formed it. Whoever set it, the task of this guardian is clear: he is meant to keep us in place after death—compare the aim of the mother's keeping—and to ensure that the dead do not wander back to disturb the living. "Peace after death" fixes tradition, assigning place at the cost of mobility. Since the dead here are poets, they are offered the esthetic inducement or charm of beholding their own works in the tapestry of imagination. And yet Stevens tells us that the dead must be guarded: ever Odyssean, they will try to escape the cave of the Cyclops in order to accomplish their return.

The "she" of canto v is a wisdom figure, indeed a goddess of wisdom, reminiscent of Yeats's early symbol of the Rose. The connection to Yeats's imagery might account for the gnomic "rosed out of prestiges / Of rose." Just as the wisdom figure leaves behind self-consciousness in her perfect selfhood, so she leaves behind the symbol or prestige of the Rose—etymologically, "prestige" derives from *praestigium*, an illusion or juggler's trick—in her attainment of knowledge. A favored word for knowledge with Stevens is "discovery," and so "She held men closely with discovery." But since this figure conducts men across the threshold, her revelation has to do with the knowledge of death:

> She was a self that knew, an inner thing,
> Subtler than look's declaiming, although she moved
>
> With a sad splendor, beyond artifice,
> Impassioned by the knowledge that she had,
> There on the edges of oblivion.

Possessing all the attributes of a muse, she nevertheless conducts to oblivion, not fame. Just as Stevens seemed to be enforcing a distinction between ultimate intellect and generations of the imagination, so he now forces us to brood on the possible discrepancy between that intellect and this "knowledge that she had." Perhaps the distinction has to do with the dissociation between intellect and selfhood. In the region of ultimate intellect, there is no longer any room for the self. So we find the wisdom figure, "a self that knew, an inner thing," on the point of extinction.

In the opening canto we are told that "the third form speaks, because the ear repeats, // Without a voice, inventions of farewell." The "flash of voice" in which she speaks comes close enough to *flesh* of voice (as in word-made-flesh) to bring out her status as *logos*. But as she says good-bye she also seems to be speeding into invisibility, detaching herself from the poet. The exhalation spoken of in the final tercet of canto V may indeed be the departing poetic breath, the poetic psyche, while the "reddened" form of the departing muse blends into the light of the setting sun. The principle of inwardness has been transformed into "a motion outward." The separation between muse and poet is marked by his use of the more distant pronoun "her" in the last line, where the logic of the vocative address leads us to expect the intimacy of "your":

> O exhalation, O fling without a sleeve
> And motion outward, reddened and resolved
> From sight, in the silence that follows her last word—

Before looking at the complex act of disengagement performed by Stevens in the concluding canto, we should try to determine where he has brought us thus far. As an elegy, "The Owl in the Sarcophagus" must present a surmise as to the shape of survival, whether literary or personal. What does this poem tell us of the beyond? The poem's dense imagery makes it seem almost crude to pose such a blunt question, but "Owl" does represent itself as a far flight of imagination. First of all, it is extremely difficult to determine the relationship between the "three forms." Stevens tells us that "peace is cousin by a hundred names," but the problem I am discussing is not a question of kinship. Are the forms linked in a temporal progression, so that we "climb" in hierarchical ascent from sleep to peace to the mother? Or is Stevens playing with the spatial concept of the urn, so that the figures simply revolve into view? Do the three figures represent competing or complementary visions of the poetic soul's fate? Are we to understand Stevens' vision as a dream-blending of all three realms? Certainly, no fully worked-out credo can be found in the poem, yet Stevens has left some rigorous clues, which I have tried to expound in my reading, to guide us in differentiating the figures and the poet's reaction to them. The state of "sleep realized," whether achieved by the quester or the dead themselves, is the state of celebration proper, since it represents the whiteness of "the ultimate intellect." All questions of individuality fade in the light of that "diamond jubilance." But when the poem goes on to ask the question Wordsworth asked in Book V of *The Prelude* concerning the "consecrated works of Bard and Sage"—"Where would they be?"[11]—the mood darkens. The canto devoted to peace unveils the ending place of imagination. We find out that the products as well as the producers (both are "generations") are preserved, but in a mausoleum. And the mother's abrupt break-off indicates another state of dead-endedness ("her last word") for the imagination.

The three figures seem to portend three separate, if not congruent, fates, depending on how one defines the essential activity of man and poet. "Sleep" foresees a future least discontinuous with the past, but constructed on the principle of visionary impersonality and immateriality. The pathos at the heart of "peace after death" comes from the realization that the material forms of art have no place in this domain, except to dress "An immaculate personage in nothingness." And yet poets cannot break the spell of their narcissistic attraction to those glittering forms. "She that says good-by" stands halfway between sleep and peace, less materially grounded than the latter, more so than the former, since her being belongs to speech. Though Stevens can foresee continuity between earthly and higher vision, speech cannot follow beyond the fire. He is not the first to make this observation, but to envision the truth of the end point oneself means experiencing it anew. So Stevens suffers the wounding force of the muse-mother's disappearance into "silence," the slashing mark of discontinuity which ends her section. Selfhood vanishes and so does the poetry of the self. If "peace after death" spells the obsolescence of our only true begettings, then the disappearance of her who sponsors selfhood removes the begetter as well. If we are to survive, Stevens seems to be saying at the end of the vision proper in "The Owl in the Sarcophagus" (the end of canto v), we will survive in the refining and self-extinguishing fire of ultimate intellect.

But it is also necessary to live in the here and now, to keep the poetic career going until the end, and so Stevens must enact the difficult return from the site of vision. The dash which concludes the fifth canto is the most radical break in all of Stevens' poetry; unlike an enticing ellipsis, it offers little room for interpretation, serving rather to divide than to bridge. The final canto seems at first to deflate what the poet has seen "there," with its talk of mythology, mufflings, and monsters:

> This is the mythology of modern death
> And these, in their mufflings, monsters of elegy,
> Of their own marvel made, of pity made,
>
> Compounded and compounded, life by life,
> These are death's own supremest images,
> The pure perfections of parental space,
>
> The children of a desire that is the will,
> Even of death, the beings of the mind
> In the light-bound space of the mind, the floreate
>   flare . . .
>
> It is a child that sings itself to sleep,
> The mind, among the creatures that it makes,
> The people, those by which it lives and dies.

Mythology is generally not a favored word in Stevens, nor is "modern" ("Of Modern Poetry" notwithstanding). The two words together can comprise something of an oxymoron. As "A Mythology Reflects Its Region" will put it: "We never lived in a time / When mythology was possible."[12] "Mufflings" make us aware that Stevens observes no faces in this poem; "the mother's face" will be unveiled only in "Auroras." (In the "Ode on Indolence" Keats addresses his three figures in these words: "How came ye muffled in so hush a masque?") "Monsters" takes us back, through etymology, to "reality is prodigy," in the first canto, since these are *monstra* or omens. There is the further implication that, as "monsters of elegy," they have somehow become outsized projections of the elegiac impulse, threatening to overburden the occasion as well as its author, were his identity clear. I add this last qualification because even though Stevens asserts that they were "Of their own marvel made, of pity made," the identity of the fashioner is problematic. This ambiguity prevails until the end in Stevens, where it informs the question of who has created the fire-fangled bird in "Of Mere Being." Clearly, these elegiac figures have not made themselves, yet they have attained a hypostatized self-sufficiency and self-identity—"of their own marvel made." So Stevens is insisting upon their status as fabrications, even while according these concepts a quasi-natural status, in that they seem native to the human mind. If they had not been invented, they would have had to exist. "Compounded and compounded, life by life," these figures are secreted out of the genius of the race. The opening four lines of canto VI represent an effort to ground the vision Stevens has borne, to anchor it in the collective mind, though we should always remember that it took one man—*a* man—to walk living among the forms of thought.

This final canto contains only one sentence and is rivaled in elusiveness only by that other single-sentence tease, "The Snow Man." The sentence may not be unreadable, but it is virtually ungraspable, as clause after clause glides into place, deferring finality for as long as possible. The chiastic structuring of these clauses makes meaning especially difficult to decide. Each cross-coupling involves another interpretive decision, one that must be made if the entire sequence of terms in this last canto is to be understood. Lines 4 through 8 in the sixth canto constitute its heart, setting up a stunning series of appositions, as clauses rock back and forth, preparing us for the lullaby of "a child that sings itself to sleep." Let us try to line up these clauses in the logical columns, straightening out the chiasmuses:

compounded and compounded	life by life
supremest images	death's own
pure perfections	parental space
the children	a desire that is the will /
the beings of the mind	even of death

In the crossing between "life by life" and "these are death's own," Stevens glides over the divide separating these states. An effacing of distinctions is the basic strategy of this method, as begetter and begotten image are blurred in our reading (as opposed to our schematic charting of the lines). Making it this hard to sort out appositives disguises the shock value of some of these equations. The asserted continuum between life and death has the ring of solace to it, but the realization that Stevens is equating death with parental space is more jolting. One is tempted to soften the statement by substituting "ancestral" for "parental," but since Stevens goes on to link "a desire that is the will" with "parental," this ameliorating gesture is difficult to justify. It is legitimate, though, to ask which parents Stevens intends: the biological or the cultural parents? Or have they merged at this point? In any case, the death wish, as Stevens sees it, seems to grow out of a desire to return to parental space, as inhabited by the consanguine characters of the poem. Return, perhaps, is not the precise word, since Stevens envisions a joining of parent and child in that space, a joining of origin and end. By calling the mind a child, Stevens blends begetter and begotten, since the child of the last tercet is no longer an esthetic offspring of the mind, but the mind itself. It has been said that men die because they cannot connect their beginning and their end; Stevens might argue that death ensues exactly at the moment of such connection, with the erasure of a saving distance between producer and product.

The poem's closing image rewards endless reading, however simple it may seem at first. What is "a child that sings itself to sleep"? On the one hand, such a child seems terribly alone, forsaken almost. And yet, a proud sense of self-sufficiency lodges in the image as well, as if the child were a solitary swan drifting off in song. Child as "childe" might be a secondary meaning at work here, giving a heroic dimension to the death song which is also a lullaby, a lyric of entrance and departure, fitting for a child who is also an old man. But the intimations of immortality aroused by this evocation of the child have already been spelled out: the prophet has been preceded by his prophecy. By proclaiming the mind's generative powers even on the verge of death, Stevens in no way evades or revises the severity of the vision he has witnessed. The emphasis upon "makes" in the penultimate line, then, becomes all the more extraordinary, since we know the ultimate fate of those begettings. The poetic will, though, simply has no choice but to continue making, for the fate of "the people" depends upon it. The creative instinct survives even the projection of its own consignment to oblivion, survives the rejection of any teleological solace for the poet and his creatures.

"To an Old Philosopher in Rome" was written some months before the actual death of Santayana in Rome, but it nevertheless seems fitting to call the poem an elegy, though at times it verges on eulogy. The poem remains "On the threshold of heaven," even in it final lines when the lifetime's design of the philosopher "is realized." To say that the poem is about dying rather than death would be one way of accounting for its utter difference in tone and vision from "The Owl in the Sarcophagus"; more to the point, I think, is the fact that Santayana was a man who gave up poetry for philosophy. As Stevens put it in a letter, "He [Santayana] had definitely decided not to be a poet."[13] Most readers will simply assume that Stevens uses Santayana as an example of what his own preparation for death should be like, but the distinction Stevens has drawn between poet and philosopher ought to be brooded upon. The central personage in "To an Old Philosopher in Rome" treats his approaching death reasonably, even in his metaphors of transformation, all of which can be clearly traced to the objects lying about him: "the blown banners change to wings"; "the newsboys' muttering / Becomes another murmuring." This discovery of the realm of "another" lacks the true *otherness* displayed in "The Owl in the Sarcophagus." But the latter is a poet's vision, not a philosopher's meditation. (I would never make such a bald assertion of difference between poetry and philosophy if I did not think that the two poems read together insist upon it.) Whatever it was about the death of Henry Church that sparked Stevens' flight of imagination, "Owl" became the vehicle for exploring what happens to the poet's creations after his death. "To an Old Philosopher in Rome" reveals no such narcissistic anxiety over the survival of the image, a fact that might be explained by the poem's emphasis on the ideality of vision, as well as its ability to exclude or repress uncertainties about the spirit's final resting place.

As a poem of declaration, "To an Old Philosopher in Rome" comes upon no startling discoveries, though its sense of poise upon the threshold ought to startle us in the wake of Stevens' visionary jaunt in "Owl." What relation exists between the two poems? Can they be complementary? Are we meant to reconsider the status of vision in "Owl," or must we regard "Santayana" (and that in Stevens which most responds to him) as holding only the noblest of illusions? "To an Old Philosopher in Rome" will probably remain the more "popular" of the two poems, and continue to be regarded as the more "orthodox" version of Stevens' beliefs, if only because its avoidance of eschatological speculation makes it the more comfortable poem to read. One effect of consigning "The Owl in the Sarcophagus" to this realm of the heretical, or peripheral, is to limit its ability to disrupt orderly notions about Stevens.

From the opening lines of "To an Old Philosopher in Rome," Stevens conveys his desire to write a less severe elegy than "The Owl in the Sarcophagus," to bridge heaven and earth rather than disrupt any continuity we might project between the realms. Choosing the unrhymed, five-line stanza over the tercet allows him to be less elliptical in his transitions. (The poem's literal ellipses are among the smoothest in all of Stevens.) Such breaks as there are come in the inevitable glide between enjambed lines—"The figures in the street / Become the figures of heaven"—where they cause no breach. The poem stops comfortably on the threshold, avoiding that searing "passage" into the beyond which gives "The Owl in the Sarcophagus" its sense of trespass and menace. Vision in "To an Old Philosopher in Rome" is governed by "parallels" and "perspective":

> The threshold, Rome, and that more merciful Rome
> Beyond, the two alike in the make of the mind.
> It is as if in a human dignity
> Two parallels become one, a perspective of which
> Men are part both in the inch and in the mile.

These plotted ratios of surmise correct the outrageous assertions of unmediated vision in "Owl": "A man walked living among the forms of thought / To see their lustre truly as it is"; "There he saw well . . ." One could go on and on in this vein, and then point again to a phrase from the third stanza of "To an Old Philosopher"—"the horizons of perception"—in order to establish what might be called the decorous sense of boundary in the later elegy, its refusal to push too far into an afterlife that might prove inhospitable to the imagination's desire. As a result, when Stevens writes here,

> The human end in the spirit's greatest reach,
> The extreme of the known in the presence of the
> extreme
> Of the unknown,

we measure words such as "greatest" and "extreme" against the cast of mind displayed in "The Owl in the Sarcophagus," and we realize that Stevens is using a different rule of mind and metaphor in this poem. Perhaps only in the lines on fire does he come close to evincing a desire to take flight:

> A light on the candle tearing against the wick
> To join a hovering excellence, to escape
> From fire and be part only of that of which
>
> Fire is the symbol: the celestial possible.

The corresponding moment in "The Owl in the Sarcophagus" is pitched in a higher rhetorical key, appropriate to the poetic quester nearing a state of identity with ultimate intellect; here, any possible identification is distanced by dependency upon the poetic trope, beautifully and exactly rendered, of the candle. *This* candle, though, will not be hypostatized into "a king as candle by our beds."

The stanzas following the invocation of fire comprise the eulogy proper, Stevens' most sustained rhetoric of praise. The delicacy of his apostrophe to the unnamed Santayana comes partly from Stevens' realization that he stands in the anomalous position of a student addressing his master. This indeed may account for "the pity that is the memorial of this room":

> Be orator but with an accurate tongue
> And without eloquence, O, half-asleep,
> Of the pity that is the memorial of this room,
>
> So that we feel, in this illumined large,
> The veritable small, so that each of us
> Beholds himself in you, and hears his voice
> In yours, master and commiserable man . . .

Stevens gently subverts Santayana's religiosity (however skeptical) by calling the reader's attention to the "commiserable man" at the center. Indeed, throughout the poem Stevens unobtrusively translates Santayana's faith into the esthetic realm, so that the emphasis in the final stanza on "the design of all *his* words," rather than God's Word, evokes no surprise. The nature of this esthetic faith rests on two noble idealizations. The first would assert the possibility of completing the career to one's satisfaction, bringing about "a kind of total grandeur at the end." The achievement of totality in "To an Old Philosopher in Rome" is seen as the fulfillment of a self that exerts its power of choice until the very end:

> It is a kind of total grandeur at the end,
> With every visible thing enlarged and yet
> No more than a bed, a chair and moving nuns,
> The immensest theatre, the pillared porch,
> The book and candle in your ambered room,
>
> Total grandeur of a total edifice,
> Chosen by an inquisitor of structures
> For himself. He stops upon this threshold,
> As if the design of all his words takes form
> And frame from thinking and is realized.

In the late lyrics surrounding "To an Old Philosopher in Rome," the prospect of completion is not regarded with such serenity, nor is the question of poetic afterlife so elided. But perhaps the philosopher receives a premonition of what his fate will be in the tolling of the bells heard from his chamber.

This brings us to the second of the idealizations I have mentioned, for the bells may be regarded as bodying forth a message about the company into which the dying philosopher will be absorbed, his version of tradition:

The bells keep on repeating solemn names
In choruses and choirs of choruses,
Unwilling that mercy should be a mystery
Of silence, that any solitude of sense
Should give you more than their peculiar chords
And reverberations clinging to whisper still.

Acceptance into the chorus is a figure for acceptance into tradition—described earlier as the urge "to join a hovering excellence"—here conceived of as having the power to vanquish the shadows of silence and solitude. This solemn order promises to perform the elegiac function of preservation, as the bells "keep on repeating solemn names" across the divide of life and death, culminating in "choruses and choirs of choruses."[14] For contrast, we might set this vision of the bells against Yeats's carilloners in *Per Amica Silentia Lunae,* those "ringers in the tower who have appointed for the hymen of the soul a passing bell." The concept of tradition as a harmonic whole, in which the solemn names are nevertheless preserved, marks the convergence of desire and vision in the poem, as well as the extent of its divergence from "The Owl in the Sarcophagus."

But the question of whose desire is being fulfilled, whose vision expressed, remains crucial to any interpretation of "To an Old Philosopher in Rome." Answering this question comes down to trying to decide the nature and extent of Stevens' identification with Santayana. No such problem exists in reading "Owl" where the man who "walked living among the forms of thought" is meant to discover the poet's own fate, however difficult to decipher. Though much less oblique on the verbal level, "To an Old Philosopher in Rome" forces us to confront the status of its vision at every turn by making the question of identification paramount but elusive.

Does Stevens privilege the stance of the old philosopher as a reflection of his own, or does he distance himself implicitly from the very figure he eulogizes? In other words, do the very terms of praise for the philosopher's way describe a set of impossibles for the poet?

Questions such as these force the interpreter to judge authenticity of voice and vision and thereby to reveal his or her deepest sense of Stevens' poetic temperament. The self-contained sphericity of "To an Old Philosopher in Rome," its commanding poise, its gestures toward totality ("a total grandeur"), all combine to give the poem an appearance of central authority, especially when read against the shorter, more fragmentary lyrics of the same period, or even when opposed to the deep ambivalences set out at length in "Owl." The fact that "To an Old Philosopher in Rome" does not literally have the last word in Stevens, but is itself survived by a number of gnomic lyrics which spill over its threshold, might be used to rebut the idea that Stevens achieved an orderly end to his career, but it does not weaken the case against his desire to sum up like Santayana, with a gesture of near self-congratulatory closure. To argue that Stevens would regard such an ending as both illusory and undesirable is to make a presumptuous claim about the poet's temperament, but I would insist that "To an Old Philosopher" forces us to assess the validity of its rhetoric—its "constant sacrament of praise," to quote "Peter Quince at the Clavier"—which returns us to the question of the poet's identification with his central figure.

As a version of the hero, Santayana is both more perfect and more human than any of Stevens' earlier models, for the proximity of death sanctifies the plainness of plain life. No disabling return of the merely ordinary is allowed to undo the philosopher's achieved position. Santayana belongs to that class of purer and narrower consciousnesses created by Stevens for the purpose of measuring his own nature against a hypothetical ideal. Sometimes the comparison generates a bad conscience, but more often than not it leaves the ideal looking rather hollow. "To an Old Philosopher in Rome" represents the subtlest case of such comparison, complicated as well by the elegiac mode. The interpreter who scans the poem for overt marks of disengagement or distancing will circle endlessly, for the dying philosopher has indeed brought about the enclosure of his own system, even at the price of controlling or limiting the horizon of perception by suppressing the prophetic element of elegy. Though in many of his late poems, Stevens prepares to encounter death as *the known*, some proleptic shadow of the uncanny generally intrudes to disturb that equipoise. By opening himself to casts of metaphorical speculation on the shape of survival, Stevens brings the inexplicable into the realm of language. Since this is precisely what the figure of Santayana will not or cannot do—since he has renounced poetry—I would judge Stevens' praise, finally, to be eulogistic of another, rather than prescriptive for himself. For the order Santayana prepares to join is not the company Stevens would keep; the poet's place is with the broken bold.

5

Last Poems

We collect ourselves . . .

Yeats is mentioned just once in Stevens' letters—appropriately enough, on the occasion of his funeral. Yeats had died in France, where his body remained throughout the war; in 1948, with great public fanfare, the remains were returned to Ireland and Drumcliffe churchyard. Stevens' Irish correspondent, Thomas McGreevy, described the occasion to him and in his reply Stevens marveled at the attention shown to the dead poet:

> In spite of Yeats' contributions to the national spirit, or, say, in spite of his additions to the national nature, it is hard to see how these ceremonies came to take on their public aspect. The transport from France on a corvette of the Navy, the procession from Galway to Sligo, the lying in state were acts of recognition and homage of a public character. Conceding that Yeats was a man of world-wide fame, it is an extraordinary thing in the modern world to find any poet being so honored. Yet the funeral of Paul Valéry

> was a great affair. Moreover, people are as much interested in Rilke as if he was human enough and, in addition, something more. The fact must be that the meaning of the poet as a figure in society is a precious meaning to those for whom it has any meaning at all. If some of those that took part in this episode did so, very likely because of the man's fame, the fact remains that his fame could not be different from his poetry.[1]

Stevens never wrote a more revealing letter. Moving from the example of Yeats to that of Valéry and Rilke, he is forced to conclude that the public does not always act blindly in the bestowal of fame and honor. The case of Yeats, a public figure, may be understandable. But then there is the fame of Rilke to consider, whom "people are as much interested in . . . as if he was human enough." And "the funeral of Paul Valéry was a great affair." So even hermetic poets can be publicly honored at their death. As Stevens neared seventy, he could regard himself as the equal of any in that illustrious trio—the American poet standing alongside the Irish, French, and German—but he also knew that his funeral would be no great affair.

"When a great poet dies, the immediate critical question is often where to bury him."[2] But as Lawrence Lipking goes on to show in *The Life of the Poet*, the true arbiters of funerary rites are the poets who come after, in whose elegies and *tombeaux* (Mallarmé is a central figure for Lipking) the dead poet receives, as well as claims, his due obsequies. The question of where to bury the poet becomes one of *how* to bury him, and both merge with the overriding concern of how to mediate, or defend against, his legacy. Only for the "public" is the poet's fate circumscribed by his tomb; for other poets, "scandal, metamorphosis, the threat of resurrection keep the tomb in flux."[3] Lipking's analyses of Mallarmé's *tombeaux* for Baudelaire and Verlaine center on these sonnets' rich and strange imagery for the shape of poetic survival.

> Two alternative images of what a poet leaves conspire in the final lines of the sonnet. On one side there is Baudelaire's "marble," the finished, perfect tomb of his life-work that celebrates his absence. Yet around that marble, circling it with shudders, a veil hovers like a miasma—the still-dangerous shadow that refuses (even syntactically) to take form. The poems of Baudelaire resist subsiding into "literature" or a final edition; instead they enter our most secret inner life. . . . Baudelaire lives on as nothing more than an ironic choice of words, a shadow in a pool of light. Only when absent can he enter us. He becomes "acutest at his vanishing."[4]
>
> Indeed, the *tombeau* denies death in many ways. Mallarmé flatly refuses any religious pieties or obituaries that would wrap Verlaine up. . . . The poem suggests that we could [escape death], partly by joining the earth in its endless changes and partly by transforming every appearance of nature into matter for poetry. Hidden in the grass and scattered into pieces, Verlaine performs the work that Mallarmé had once told him was the poet's sole duty: "The Orphic explanation of the Earth."[5]

The poems from Stevens' last phase—everything from 1950 onward—can all be considered versions of the *tombeau* in that they devise figures for the poet's own legacy after death, and do so without the "occasional" mediation of another poet's passing. All poets become to some degree their own veiled elegists; but the length of Stevens' career, his inexhaustible speculativeness, and the distrust he displayed toward the institutions of literature by remaining an outsider, combined to give his last poems an air of prolonged, idiosyncratic meditation on the poet's death rarely matched in English. In "The Rock," the presence of the tomb is made explicit, whereas most of the lyrics from this period inhabit a landscape so pervaded with end signs as to make the objectification, or even the mention, of death redundant. Nor is death really the issue for Stevens; what concerns him is the end of imagination, its destination and duration. What form does it take upon death? In the hypothetical air of these questions, Stevens' extravagant metaphors for the forms of farewell take on a strongly literal character, which explains why these late lyrics strike readers as both distant and preternaturally close:

> Distant, yet close enough to wake
> The chords above your bed to-night.[6]

These spatial metaphors express the yoking together of the farfetched and the ordinary in Stevens' late poetry, the homely and the *unheimlich*, the transcendent and the immanent. Another way of putting this is to say that Stevens familiarizes tropes of the otherworldly. As Frank Kermode says in an essay which demonstrates the importance of the "dwelling" in both Stevens and Heidegger: "The voyager easily passes into the unfamiliar—into death—as if it were the known."[7] And yet it would be wrong to imply that Stevens achieves—or even intends—resolution in these poems, for no unified vision of the imagination's end can be deduced from the perspectives of the last phase. While the momentary fusion of opposites ("Distant, yet close enough") portends a kind of perfection, the late lyrics as a group seem to be aimed against the very idea of satisfactory closure, as if Stevens were returning to the improvisational mode of the *Harmonium* "fragment," now coupled with a style best described as a fusion of simplicity and intensity.

To keep the poetic career an ongoing activity, a poet such as Stevens *must* forestall premature closure. The dual vision of the late poems arises from the mingling of this need to continue and the desire for rest and reward—the poet's reward, that species of immortality called fame. The poet must court and fight off canonization; he must celebrate what he has accomplished and disparage it; view poetry sub specie aeternitatis and as the most fragile, provisional activity, in need of daily renewal. Edward Said declares that, for the modernists, "in writing there is no longer any proper starting or stopping, only activity renewed or interrupted—and this because for the self there is no starting or stopping, only a selfhood resumed or interrupted."[8] Consequently, the idea of poetic vocation in modernity is replaced by the all-embracing concept of a poetic career whose boundaries must be fixed by the poet himself. "Whereas the former [i.e., vocation] required taking certain memorial steps and imitating a ritual progress, in the latter [career] the writer had to create not only his art but the very course of his writing."[9] No poet makes us feel this more acutely than Stevens. His independence from the normal economic pressures of the literary life made him that much more responsible for forging "the very course of his writing."

Stevens' last phase is complicated by his desire to stand outside his career, even as he adds to the "total edifice" of his work. The quoted phrase comes from the ending of "To an Old Philosopher in Rome." The paean to Santayana presents a comforting vision of the whole career falling into place with the addition of this final stone:

> Total grandeur of a total edifice,
> Chosen by an inquisitor of structures
> For himself. He stops upon this threshold,
> As if the design of all his words takes form
> And frame from thinking and is realized.

As I said in the previous chapter, I do not believe that this is the authentic voice of Stevens at the end. Desire to pay homage to the philosopher, or even to capture Santayana's (not his own) serenity, may have guided Stevens' rhetoric here. But the best and most intriguing of the final poems aim not to complete the career so much as to prolong it by keeping the vital poetic spirit alive. Sometimes this involves turning against the completed forms of art belonging to one's own past (especially the appearance of a *Collected Poems*) in a revisionary movement similar to the *retractio*. Disparaging what has already been fashioned clears ground for new work, besides testing the resiliency of the completed artifact by seeing if it can withstand the onslaught of its maker's repudiation. Sometimes Stevens aims to revise the strengths of his past work, sometimes its perceived weaknesses; so the late poems will astonish us by turns with their confessions of impotence and unbridled power. And there are moments when Stevens appears to spurn the material vestments of art altogether in the effort to recognize his own spirit. Whitman's late poem "A Clear Midnight" was a precious poem for Stevens,[10] and it might serve as a prototype for some of the late lyrics:

> This is thy hour, O soul, thy free flight into the
> wordless,
> Away from books, away from art, the day erased, the
> lesson done,
> Thee fully forth emerging, silent, gazing, pondering the
> themes thou lovest best,
> Night, sleep, death and the stars.

If Stevens at times seems capable of taking this free flight away from books into the wordless empyrean, it is because he has so thoroughly internalized literary tradition. At the same time, the degree of self-allusiveness in the last poems indicates that there may be no tradition for this poet outside of his own works. For Stevens, tradition resides within his oeuvre, rather than the other way around. Survival of the literary self and survival of the tradition become synonymous. Yet what institution can guarantee the survival of such a quicksilver spirit? The implicit program of these late lyrics instructs us that only the ever-active imagination can project and preserve the forms of literary immortality, even in repose.

In "The Rock," Stevens stands at the end of his allotted three score and ten years. The rock may very well be the tomb of the past, since the houses of the past loom like gravestones:

It is an illusion that we were ever alive,
Lived in the houses of mothers, arranged ourselves
By our own motions in a freedom of air.

Regard the freedom of seventy years ago.
It is no longer air. The houses still stand,
Though they are rigid in rigid emptiness.

Even our shadows, their shadows, no longer remain.
The lives these lived in the mind are at an end.
They never were . . . The sounds of the guitar

Were not and are not. Absurd. The words spoken
Were not and are not. It is not to be believed.
The meeting at noon at the edge of the field seems like

An invention, an embrace between one desperate clod
And another in a fantastic consciousness,
In a queer assertion of humanity:

A theorem proposed between the two—
Two figures in a nature of the sun,
In the sun's design of its own happiness . . .

The opening eight lines of "The Rock" have an engraved quality, but they are not meant to be a celebratory epitaph. Stevens surveys "the freedom of seventy years ago," a period which now must seem very dead to him indeed. He is, in effect, surveying his natural life span, the life lived in the houses of mothers. Childhood and its freedoms "no longer remain," as the elegiac formula runs. In the opening lines of the poem, Stevens looks at the external signs and scenes of his early life, looks at them with the outer eye, and they appear dead to him. Even their intimations, their "shadows," are gone.

When the ellipsis comes after "They never were," it strikes us almost as a release from the rigors of finality, especially after the epitaphic solemnity of the preceding periods. "They never were . . ." trails off, but also leads to a new train of thought. Once again, Stevens appears to be saying farewell to an idea. In this case, the ellipsis leads to a turn from external to internal lives, or better yet from the natural world to the world of culture or poetry. Beholding the outward signs of his own lived life, Stevens declares them to be dead: "The lives these lived in the mind are at an end." (One might quibble and point out that Stevens says only "an end," which is better than the finality of *the* end.) The ellipsis leads to the more disturbing consideration of whether the *inward* signs of life and continuity still remain. To test this, Stevens returns to his touchstones. "The sounds of the guitar," we remember from "An Ordinary Evening in New Haven," are the sounds of Stevens' muse, an emblem of faith and continuity, a hedge against forgetfulnes. Now, especially, he needs something to keep him from forgetting. So Stevens tests the proposition that the sounds of the guitar never even existed, and finds that proposition absurd. "The words spoken," a trope for poetry, are emblems of the same order as the guitar sounds. It is interesting to observe Stevens shy away from associating poetry with material signs, such as "houses." One might suspect that he would crave the materiality these offer, but "The Rock" shows us how such signs can petrify. The perseverance of the guitarist and his essential, abstract chords, which remind one of what Frost termed the "sentence sound,"[11] are more comforting.

Although remembrance of these elements of fidelity begins to turn the poem and the mood around, Stevens needs something still more essential in order to lift the tomblike weight of the past. "The meeting at noon at the edge of the field" is an act of erotic consummation which, even in memory, still has the power to revivify. The weight this memory must lift is ponderous, even without the obstacles Stevens piles up through his almost deliberately deflating terms: the lovers are "desperate clods," coming together in "a queer assertion of humanity"; at best, they achieve an "impermanence" in nature's "permanent cold." Here Stevens tests the strength of this memory and this experience, trying to weight it down "with the great weightings of the end," as the poem "Madame La Fleurie" will later put it. These weightings, however, can be lightened, along the lines of that "weight we lift with the finger of a dream, / The heaviness we lighten by light will," to quote from "Ordinary Evening." In "The Rock," Stevens sees this process in terms of a blossoming:

> an illusion so desired
>
> That the green leaves came and covered the high rock,
> That the lilacs came and bloomed, like a blindness
> cleaned,
> Exclaiming bright sight, as it was satisfied,
>
> In a birth of sight. The blooming and the musk
> Were being alive, an incessant being alive,
> A particular of being, that gross universe.

This description of the green leaves coming forth puts one in mind of Keats's stricture about poetry: "if Poetry comes not as naturally as the Leaves to a tree it had better not come at all."[12] The erotic rendezvous seems to be the spark that brings the sounds of the guitar and the words spoken fully to life. Whatever the ordering, Stevens is elaborating another trinity: music, words, the object of desire.

When all come together, we have nothing less than "a birth of sight." This birth amounts to the *second* birth, the birth into poetry, and Stevens sets it against the birth into nature of seventy years ago. Many of the relics from the first "no longer remain" in the mind, but the emblems of the second still comprise—extraordinary phrase—"an incessant being alive." The poet who began this section by wondering if we were *ever* alive has brought himself around to the recognition of an unending, inward life—which is not to say that his pathos at losing the outward signs of the past has been diminished.

But Stevens declares, at the opening of "*The Poem as Icon*," that "it is not enough to cover the rock with leaves." This means both that Stevens is not interested in covering the rock—he wants an uncovering, a disclosure, an apocalypse, for to disclose the rock fully would be to cure it—and also, somehow more surprising, that to cover with *leaves* is not enough. As we read on in "The Rock," we see that Stevens demands more from the "green leaves"; they must be "more than leaves that cover the barren rock." We must ingest the fruit of these leaves:

> And yet the leaves, if they broke into bud,
> If they broke into bloom, if they bore fruit,
>
> And if we ate the incipient colorings
> Of their fresh culls might be a cure of the ground.

Stevens undoes the mock disclaimer of thirty years before in "Le Monocle de Mon Oncle": "I know no magic trees, no balmy boughs, / No silver-ruddy, gold-vermilion fruits." What makes the magic even more remarkable here is the insistence on the necessity of eating the fruit, for this amounts to a further internalization of what is already an inner thing, "the fiction of the leaves." Something of the feeling we get at the close of Keats's "Ode to Psyche," a feeling of falling deeper and deeper into mental recesses, occurs at this point.

But even as we are asked to absorb the fruit of the leaves, a certain rigidity in the conception of those leaves sets in. Stevens begins to see the poem as an icon:

> The fiction of the leaves is the icon
> Of the poem, the figuration of blessedness,
> And the icon is the man.

In "*Seventy Years Later*," the presence of the poem was signified by the sounds of the guitar and the words spoken; now these are replaced by the icon. Is this a reductive movement? By the end of "*The Poem as Icon*," Stevens will claim that the poem brings "mixed motion" to the rock, but we generally do not think of icons in terms of motion. An icon usually denotes nonrepresentational figuration, and as "The Rock" goes on, "the fiction of the leaves" becomes increasingly removed from any natural corollary:

> They bud and bloom and bear their fruit without change.
> They are more than leaves that cover the barren rock.

A price must be paid for the attainment of iconic status; other functions of poetry are subsumed, just as the very word "icon" hovers over the second section of the poem. (The epitaphic or engraved character of the lines throughout "The Rock" also reinforces the sense of the iconic.) And yet by having us eat the incipient colorings, Stevens suggests that we take communion, take the iconic substance into ourselves. This becomes the taking of the cure.

If the assertion that "the fiction of the leaves is the icon of the poem" raises questions about ascetic reductiveness, then what about the claim that "the icon is the man"? The phrase strikes directly against the earlier self surveyed at the beginning of the poem, the self who once "lived in the houses of mothers." More darkly, perhaps, the freedom of having "arranged ourselves / By our own motions in a freedom of air" also departs. Icons are not free in that sense. In curing the rock, the icon takes on something of its character; the man who becomes the icon loses his merely natural history. This may very well be the price paid for literary survival. For Stevens—however cautiously, however hedged with qualifiers—is proclaiming a kind of deification in "The Rock." Wedged between "The fiction of the leaves is the icon / Of the poem," and "the icon is the man" stands "the figuration of blessedness" with its suggestion that both icon and man are blessed figures.

In "The Rock," Stevens rather conspicuously omitted winter from his garland of fictional leaves "that cover the rock":

> the pearled chaplet of spring,
> The magnum wreath of summer, time's autumn snood,
> Its copy of the sun, these cover the rock.

But "A Discovery of Thought" finds a cure for winter in "an antipodal, far-fetched creature," born out of the winter cold itself. The poem opens on a note of grim, almost incapacitating beauty. After the repetitions of "cure" in "The Rock," it is startling to discover a first stanza ending on the word "sickness":

At the antipodes of poetry, dark winter,
When the trees glitter with that which despoils them,
Daylight evaporates, like a sound one hears in sickness.

These glittering trees, standing out against the black wintry sky, are an earthly equivalent of the diamond cabala, or crown, of "Auroras." They represent the beauty of extinguishings, the force of the mysterious power Stevens can refer to only as "that which," a pronominal phrase one begins to find in these late poems.

As in "Auroras," prostration takes the form of a return to childhood:

One is a child again. The gold beards of waterfalls
Are dissolved as in an infancy of blue snow.
It is an arbor against the wind, a pit in the mist . . .

But as the favored images of childhood, the Wordsworthian spots of time, recur in memory, Stevens feels the influx of a new power, or wild surmise:

One thinks that it could be that the first word
    spoken . . .
One thinks, when the houses of New England catch the
    first sun,

The first word would be of the susceptible being arrived,
The immaculate disclosure of the secret no more
    obscured.

"Susceptible being arrived" is a virtual echo of "incessant being alive," the powerful phrase which Stevens used to deny the death of memory in "*Seventy Years Later*." Since the "susceptible being" is born into or within "A Discovery of Thought," just as an "incessant being alive" arrived after the "birth of sight" represented by the coming of the wished-for leaves, it is fair to say that this new being is also designed to ward off death. And indeed the child arrives "pronouncing its new life and ours." This new life that will be "ours" is as close as Stevens ever comes to beseeching a renewal bordering on resurrection. The child embodies an "immaculate disclosure"—a revelation, an apocalyptic uncovering. The winter setting, so full of personal meaning for Stevens as to be virtually his own season, is nevertheless also a "traditional" setting for the birth of a redeemer: "It was the winter wild, / When the heaven-born child . . ."

A closer analogue for this "susceptible being," so closely linked to the emblems of childhood, comes in the phrase Hart Crane used in "Passages" to describe the second birth: "an improved infancy." In Stevens this becomes a creature "worthy of birth." The poet either gives birth to, or predicts the coming of, this worthy successor, the miraculous embodiment of the poet's own will to survive:

> The accent of deviation in the living thing
> That is its life preserved, the effort to be born
> Surviving being born, the event of life.

The severe compression of these lines gives new energy to the idea that the poet can create his own progeny. We must remind ourselves that Stevens has literalized the trope of the figurative child, for everything said in these lines can also apply to the poem as "living thing." "Deviation," considered as metaphor (Bloom points us to canto IX of "Ordinary Evening," where Stevens mentions "trope or deviation"), preserves life by turning it aside or away from the mortal poet. The living thing, unlike the living man, does not die. The middle clause in this triad of attributes—"the effort to be born / Surviving being born"—yields the most to meditation. As in the scenario of second birth sketched in "Esthétique," canto x—"Being born / Again"—enjambment creates a divide between the two births, spiritual and natural. "The effort to be born / Surviving being born" points to poetry as an ongoing, vital activity which survives the death-in-life of ordinary existence. The implicit argument, unmatched in Stevens for the severity of its program, is that only by truly surviving our birth can we hope to survive death. To consider the figure-made-literal, the actual child in the scene, so hypostatizes the argument as to make it virtually unthinkable. "Deviation," again, should remind us that no simple identity between the poet and this "antipodal, far-fetched creature" can be posited, just as the poet and his poems are not identical. A saving element of the irrational, the unknowable, prevails in such deviation, so although "A Discovery of Thought" predicts "The immaculate disclosure of the secret no more obscured," it stops short of representing that discovery. Only the "event of life" can disclose the secret.

On the one hand, then, Stevens is projecting a worthy successor, an heir, whose nativity is continuous with Stevens' own native season, winter. And yet the creature comes from "afar," bearing "a new life." The child is both miraculous and "susceptible," presumably to "our desire for speech and meaning." If we think of winter as an epoch, not merely a season, then the wider implications of such a birth ally the poem to another great lyric of nativity: "The Second Coming." Stevens' vision is a possible answer, or antidote, to Yeats's nightmare of "the rough beast," as the second birth shades into a new version of the second coming.

The high, consolatory rhetoric of "The Rock" is scarcely over before Stevens sets himself to revise it. Written almost simultaneously with "The Rock," "The Course of a Particular" opens with a shock: "Today the leaves cry." What happened to the fiction of the leaves and their Aesculapian powers of healing? "The final found, / The plenty of the year and of the world" from "The Rock" now becomes "the final finding of the ear," which concerns and cures no one at all:

Today the leaves cry, hanging on branches swept by
    wind,
Yet the nothingness of winter becomes a little less.
It is still full of icy shades and shapen snow.

The leaves cry . . . One holds off and merely hears the
    cry.
It is a busy cry, concerning someone else.
And though one says that one is part of everything,

There is a conflict, there is a resistance involved;
And being part is an exertion that declines:
One feels the life of that which gives life as it is.

The leaves cry. It is not a cry of divine attention,
Nor the smoke-drift of puffed-out heroes, nor human cry.
It is the cry of leaves that do not transcend themselves,

In the absence of fantasia, without meaning more
Than they are in the final finding of the ear, in the thing
Itself, until, at last, the cry concerns no one at all.

The only apparent gratification from this revision might come from the sense that Stevens has escaped the iconic status of "The Rock"; he is alive again in a "Today," even if life appears to be dwindling. Read in the context of "The Course of a Particular," "The Rock" seems to be a premature memorial, a too-early sanctification of the poetic self. Stevens returns to the world of loss announced in the opening section of "The Rock," before the cure of the leaves was taken: "The lives these lived in the mind are at an end." There is little consolation in "The Course of a Particular" and no healing; instead, the poem locates itself "in the absence of fantasia," a landscape missing precisely that desired illusion which sparked the lovers in "*Seventy Years Later*" to assert their humanity.

Any reading of "The Course of a Particular" lives or dies on the poem's second line. "Yet the nothingness of winter becomes a little less" is as quietly outrageous a statement as Stevens ever made. How can nothingness become a little *less*? We make sense of the line only because "nothing" has a long history in Stevens; he has accustomed us to play with its meanings. If "the nothingness of winter becomes a little less," then it follows that the somethingness, or quiddity, of winter increases; or the special virtue of nothingness, its negative power, is on the wane. Of simple winter misery, there is no letup: "the leaves cry, hanging on branches swept by wind." In my discussion of "Esthétique du Mal," canto III, I pointed out the unsettling effect that the gallowslike image of hanging has on Stevens: it is indeed a sign of damnation. How does this sign accord with the lessening of winter's nothingness?

I think the key to this paradox lies in the poem to which "The Course of a Particular" responds, over a distance of more than thirty years. The crying of leaves in "The Snow Man" is borne by the sound of misery:

> misery in the sound of the wind,
> In the sound of a few leaves,
>
> Which is the sound of the land
> Full of the same wind
> That is blowing in the same bare place.

To become a snow man with a mind of winter, one must hold off and merely hear the sound of misery. But in the last stanza of "The Snow Man," the poet has become a "listener,"

> who listens in the snow,
> And, nothing himself, beholds
> Nothing that is not there and the nothing that is.

By listening to the cry of the leaves, the cry of the land, Stevens was able "to behold"—the verb is as crucial as its objects—two versions of nothing. The first, "nothing that is not there," corresponds to "the absence of fantasia." But beyond or through that emerges a more powerful "nothing," a force defined positively as "the nothing that is." From this influx of negative energy flows the power to behold. Or, perhaps, the power to behold summons the discovery of "the nothing." In either case, that power comes from the trial of listening to the misery of the leaves without succumbing to pathos. "Behold" is a term we associate with prophetic contexts, and "The Snow Man" shows Stevens brought to the testing ground—the prophetic locus, the "same bare place"—in order to listen and to behold. The "wind" that blows through the land also blows through him, and the revelation of negativity is both won and bestowed, if only for the prophetic moment.

"The Course of a Particular" is a far quieter poem. No rushing wind, or spiritus, blows through the poem; mentioned in the opening line, "wind" (not *the* wind) stays there. The cry of the leaves, though heard throughout the poem, never rises in intensity. Whereas "The Snow Man" builds to power through the aggrandizement of repetition, coupled with the turning of short verses, the reiterations of "the leaves cry" does not magnify that irreducible sound, partly because of the poem's long, frequently end-stopped lines. Even the eye has dimmed somewhat: "icy shades and shapen snow" reports less than "pine-trees crusted with snow," "junipers shagged with ice," "spruces rough in the distant glitter." The effort to behold has turned into a holding off. And since so many of Stevens' late poems end with vocal epiphanies, the absence of voice here marks the poem's crisis as especially acute. "Esthétique du Mal," for example, ends with "the reverberating psalm, the right chorale"; "Auroras" closes with the rabbi's voice as he reads to the congregation; "The Owl in the Sarcophagus" gives us "a child that sings itself to sleep"; even "Ordinary Evening," in its final canto, explores sounds, words, speech, statement; and "The Rock" closes on "night's hymn of the rock." But in "The Course of a Particular," voice dwindles to cry and cry goes unanswered.

The poem's silence and the drift of its long lines reinforce the sense of entropy made explicit in "Being part [poet?] is an exertion that declines." More than the end of one poet is at stake here; the sequence, or line, that we call tradition seems to be petering out. One reason for the great power of "The

Snow Man" has to do with Stevens' sense that he is standing in a line of seers; others have stood in that "same bare place." "The Course of a Particular" focuses on the other end of tradition, on the poet's legacy to those who come after. So Stevens at first asserts that "It is a busy cry, concerning someone else." Let the next in line attend to the cry. But by the end of the poem, "The cry concerns no one at all." Perhaps there *is* no successor.

What supplants the sustaining concept of tradition is the apprehension of a force behind life itself: "One feels the life of that which gives life as it is." In "Final Soliloquy of the Interior Paramour," a poem written at the same time as "The Course of a Particular," this mysterious "that"—perhaps we should call it "that which"—is sensed in the following way:

> We feel the obscurity of an order, a whole,
> A knowledge, that which arranged the rendezvous.

It seems as if the business of poetry, this late in Stevens' life and career, has become the feeling-out of the giver, or arranger. "Final Soliloquy" presents a more generous interpretation of this obscure spirit. The monosyllabic line from "The Course of a Particular" refuses to be inflected by feeling, but in moving beyond exertion to a giver of life on its own terms, Stevens seems to be approaching a threshold beyond which his own exertions, his poems, are no longer necessary. Moving beyond the "cry" into the region of "life as it is," Stevens puts exertion aside and allows himself to sense the given. "Life as it is," in this formulation, will resemble the region glimpsed in "Of Mere Being"—"Beyond the last thought . . . on the edge of space." But here in 1950, Stevens seems to regard the region as devoid of fantasia, tending toward the blankness of literalism. No "fire-fangled" bird sits, much less sings, in the palms. The apprehension of a giver of life in "The Course of a Particular" brings no joy to Stevens, since that life-giver seems to require an end to our own imaginings. One hears the resistance involved in the standoffish tones of "One feels the life of that which gives life as it is." If Stevens is no longer a part of everything around him, he is still not yet a part of life as it is, although by the end of the poem he seems to have practiced the necessary self-extinction. Successive poems, however, are designed to resuscitate the dying fantasia. "Final Soliloquy of the Interior Paramour," for example, projects a more continuous fate for the imagination as it leaves the living, or vital, boundary of the mind.

Must we appeal to other poems for extrication from this feeling of dead-endedness? Does the poem itself offer no way out? One could point to the dialectical intensity generated by the response to "The Snow Man" as an argument against real decline. As a last resort, the acuity of writing in "The Course of a Particular" might be adduced as testament to the survival of poetic strength. But that creates a gap between style and subject. A better approach might lie in a scrutiny of what is perhaps the poem's most anomalous word: "Today." Nowhere else in Stevens do we find the word so starkly foregrounded. And coming just after "The Rock," whose transcendent consolations seemed to abolish the very ground of "Today," its appearance is doubly surprising. The word reminds us, first of all, that poetry is a daily, provisional activity. Of course poems bind each other across time, but each day also promises a new beginning—or ending. Each day is open to victory or defeat. The diminishing course of exertion in "The Course of a Particular" is, then, bound by "Today" and, instead of signaling the end of a poetic career, reasserts the poet's daily activity as constitutive of that career. I am not denying that this particular day is an ominous one, a day in which all sorts of beliefs are darkly threatened. But when a poet loses his fear he ceases to be a poet. In this sense, Stevens has more to fear from the lotuslike leaves of "The Rock" than from these "leaves that do not transcend themselves."

In the calendar of Stevens' last phase, "The Plain Sense of Things" comes after "The Course of a Particular," for now there are no leaves left hanging, no leaves left to cry:

> After the leaves have fallen, we return
> To a plain sense of things. It is as if
> We had come to an end of the imagination,
> Inanimate in an inert savoir.

Not surprisingly, in the poems of 1952 Stevens is obsessed with fallen things. "Lebensweisheitspielerei" opens: "Weaker and weaker the sunlight falls"; in "The Hermitage at the Centre," "The leaves on the macadam make a noise." Back in "Le Monocle de Mon Oncle," Stevens could celebrate the natural process or cycle that returned us "rotting back to ground":

> This luscious and impeccable fruit of life
> Falls, it appears, of its own weight to earth . . .
> An apple serves as well as any skull
> To be the book in which to read a round,
> And is as excellent, in that it is composed
> Of what, like skulls, comes rotting back to ground.

No mask of esthetic impersonality can now disguise the consequences of this fall: Stevens is already too close to "an end of the imagination," however it will end, to celebrate mere natural process. The return announced in the opening line of "Plain Sense" returns us to no source of power, it would seem, no potent origin. Once again, the fiction of the leaves is exposed.

Most disturbing, however, is the way the poem tries almost programmatically to undo, in its short space, the strength uncovered in the penultimate canto of "An Ordinary Evening in New Haven." The phrase "plain sense of things" is a hit at the "eye's plain version," but reading canto XXX of the earlier poem alongside "The Plain Sense of Things" shows the degree to which every new poem of Stevens' last phase is a response to some earlier version of the scene:

The last leaf that is going to fall has fallen.
The robins are là-bas, the squirrels, in tree-caves,
Huddle together in the knowledge of squirrels.

The wind has blown the silence of summer away.
It buzzes beyond the horizon or in the ground:
In mud under ponds, where the sky used to be reflected.

The barrenness that appears is an exposing.
It is not part of what is absent, a halt
For farewells, a sad hanging on for remembrances.

It is a coming on and a coming forth.
The pines that were fans and fragrances emerge,
Staked solidly in a gusty grappling with rocks.

The glass of the air becomes an element—
It was something imagined that has been washed away.
A clearness has returned. It stands restored.

It is not an empty clearness, a bottomless sight.
It is a visibility of thought,
In which hundreds of eyes, in one mind, see at once.

No "gusty grappling" with the elemental bareness of winter takes place in "The Plain Sense of Things"; Stevens indeed faces a season of absence and farewells. There is a world of difference between "A clearness has returned" and "we return / To a plain sense of things," between "something imagined that has been washed away" and "an end of the imagination." In 1952, Stevens is less sure what will return with the coming of winter, less sure of the renewal attendant upon even the grimmest of seasonal changes.

In a further instance of revision, Stevens confesses his growing "difficulty" by measuring his current state against another crescendo from "Ordinary Evening." When Stevens writes: "It is difficult even to choose the adjective / For this blank cold," he laments his inability, now, to live up to the task as spelled out in canto XIV of "Ordinary Evening":

He seeks

God in the object itself, without much choice.
It is a choice of the commodious adjective
For what he sees, it comes in the end to that:

The description that makes it divinity, still speech
As it touches the point of reverberation—not grim
Reality but reality grimly seen.

Yes, grim reality, Stevens seems to say in "The Plain Sense of Things": an unhappy people in a happy world, we are bent by "this sadness without a cause." Weighed against his long poems of even the recent past and their large rallyings of the spirit, "The Plain Sense of Things" seems almost to court the sense of being too weak to live up to past victories. Stevens indulges in the great poet's right of *retractio* and disparagement: "The great structure has became a minor house"; "a fantastic effort has failed." In a number of his last poems, Stevens seems intent on disparaging his career, as if to test the resiliency of his poetry to withstand attack. Can his work survive the onslaught of its maker's revulsion? Part of the test involves discovering whether his poetic spirit still lives. Is the career over or not? And if it is, can the poet rejoice in past power which is now denied him? Writing against the weight of his own past accomplishments, Stevens needs to disparage what he has done if he is to go on and do more. As an outsider, seemingly hostile to the institutions of poetry throughout his odd career, Stevens always had to push on and validate his identity as a poet on a day-to-day basis. Nearing the end of his career, Stevens is even more reluctant to entrust his identity to what he has already fashioned. So these late poems often have to clear new space for themselves at the cost of disparaging or revising the earlier work. Surveying the withered scene in "The Plain Sense of Things," Stevens recoils from the exertion it would take to find energy in the scene, even though that exertion in the presence of the minimal so often marked his characteristic triumphs of the past.

Of course, "The Plain Sense of Things" does work up to a recovery of sorts. Stevens cannot actively forego the deeply ingrained pattern of disillusionment and recovery which accounts for so much of his poetic dialectic:

> Yet the absence of the imagination had
> Itself to be imagined . . .
> Required as a necessity requires.

In the startling figure at the end of the poem—the "silence of a rat come out to see"—Stevens reaches the nadir of ironic renunciation, drastically curtailing the apotheosis of sight which closed canto xxx of "Ordinary Evening": "It is a visibility of thought, / In which hundreds of eyes, in one mind, see at once." "The Plain Sense of Things" bids at least temporary farewell to this mode of visionary or voluptuous seeing. And yet, for some readers, the picture of the lone rat, a survivor of sorts, indulging his minimal inquisitiveness, might be an even more convincing emblem than the hallucinatory magnification of the eye in "Ordinary Evening." The rat is, after all, "the grey particular" spoken of in "The Rock" (or the "grey alive," to use a phrase from the "Hades" section of *Ulysses*). The rat is also proof that "the absence of the imagination had / Itself to be imagined," since the creature, as an invention, adds to the scene while also providing the lone pair of eyes to witness the desolation. On the level of Stevensian self-allusion, the rat is a figure of minimal imal inquisitiveness, might be an even more convincing emblem than the hallucinatory magnifica- bring back some of the imagination's full force.

In "A Quiet Normal Life" Stevens comes at last—though this will not, of course, be the final time—to "place" himself: "His place, as he sat and as he thought . . ." Years ago, he placed a jar in Tennessee, but now it is a question of fixing his own place.

What does Stevens mean by "place"? The word has overtones of finality: choosing a resting place, as it were, whether in a tomb or in the vault of literary history. On the other hand, "as he sat and as he thought" describes a living place which Stevens now occupies—the room of meditation. As a synecdoche for the ongoing activity of his imagination, "as he sat and as he thought" becomes also the *subject* of Stevens' poetry. Place thus becomes topos, or commonplace. In this regard, one thinks of "The House Was Quiet and the World Was Calm" as a characteristic statement of how Stevens sat and thought. But the verve of that earlier poem, its completed dance of identifications between reader and summer night, is missing here, for "A Quiet Normal Life" is a poem of retraction, not of identification. What Stevens casts doubt upon, or retracts, is once again the value of his earlier creations:

> His place, as he sat and as he thought, was not
> In anything that he constructed, so frail,
> So barely lit, so shadowed over and naught,
>
> As, for example, a world in which, like snow,
> He became an inhabitant, obedient
> To gallant notions on the part of cold.

Stevens appears to be attacking himself at a moment of supreme strength, since the above lines can only refer to "The Snow Man." It is possible that Stevens is not criticizing the earlier work so much as confessing his present inability to see the power in it. In any event, he offers a rather passive reading of "The Snow Man" in these lines. At this distance, he can see only the "obedient" or self-extinguishing side of the poem, not its subsequent ascension to power. There is a shrewder, if more self-lacerating, logic to the assertion that he was obedient to "gallant notions on the part of cold," a striking admission of erotic preference for the cold-blooded world of art.

The second movement of this short lyric attempts to move the poem from past to present. When Stevens declares that "It was here," referring to his place, he of course means us to believe that his lyric career is ongoing:

> It was here. This was the setting and the time
> Of year. Here in his house and in his room,
> In his chair, the most tranquil thought grew peaked.

The lyric poem's place is always "here," in the lyric present, but that present is also always past: "It was here." The second movement is written to show Stevens and us that he is still alive, that his heart is still warm. In his own lexicon, there is a gain in moving from the gallant advances of the cold to the gallant advances of the warm night:

> the oldest and the warmest heart was cut
> By gallant notions on the part of night—
> Both late and alone, above the crickets' chords,
>
> Babbling, each one, the uniqueness of its sound.
> There was no fury in transcendent forms.
> But his actual candle blazed with artifice.

These lines hardly add up to a recantation on Stevens part of his own esthetic premises. The recantation of the opening stanzas served to heat the poet up again. Stevens opened "A Quiet Normal Life" by declaring that his place was not in anything that he had constructed, but the poem ends by acknowledging, with quiet but fierce pride, that "his actual candle blazed with artifice." The poem's argument, then, appears to be directed against completed art, which Stevens associates with "transcendent forms." (So much for the opening characterization of his oeuvre as "frail.")

"A Quiet Normal Life" leaves us with the sense of a poet deriving little comfort from the fact that he has fashioned transcendent, or lasting, works of art. Only the living creation of the moment blazes for him. The poem shows us the necessity of constantly recanting one's earlier work in order to create anew; yet at the same time, it shows how the poet is bound to that work for the very terms of his discourse. "Gallant notions on the part of cold," a rejected stance, leads to the repetition with a difference of "gallant notions on the part of night." Stevens is fighting off canonization—his place, and his placing by others—for the sake of preserving his living flame. At this late stage of his life and career there can be no question of escaping from art into a quiet normal life, since there can be no life for Stevens without artifice. The rejection of constructed work results only in another act of construction, another stone, soon to become cold, added to the total edifice. Merely by sitting and thinking, the Bishop prepares his tomb in Hartford.

"Final Soliloquy of the Interior Paramour" can be read as a companion piece to "A Quiet Normal Life," though composed two years earlier. The poem begins with an image of the interplay between poverty and grandeur which we find in so many of Stevens' late poems:

> Light the first light of evening, as in a room
> In which we rest and, for small reason, think
> The world imagined is the ultimate good.

Stevens is lighting a simple candle and igniting a star. If we choose to consider the light as a candle, we still cannot be sure whether this is a candle lit in a dining room, or whether it is lit for the dead. More than one intimation of finality assails the poem. The shawl Stevens mentions seems like a Yeatsian shroud, stitched for the poet's deathbed:

> Within a single thing, a single shawl
> Wrapped tightly round us, since we are poor, a warmth,
> A light, a power, the miraculous influence.

Stevens' sense of the end lies behind what is probably a scarcely concealed allusion to the feared but inevitable publication of his collected poems;

> It is in that thought that we collect ourselves,
> Out of all the indifferences, into one thing.

The appearance of a *Collected Poems* was an event Stevens resisted, for even as it signaled the desired unity of his creation, it also marked the absorption of his work into the past. As the master poet nears death, he is ever more capable of believing that he has fashioned himself into "one thing." And yet there is a price to be paid for this attainment of unity:

> Here, now, we forget each other and ourselves.
> We feel the obscurity of an order, a whole,
> A knowledge, that which arranged the rendezvous.

The moment of lyric wholeness brings on a kind of self-forgetfulness, as all that is accidental drops away from the poet. Even the "interior paramour" seems on the point of fading away. The ironies here are profound. At the very point when literary fame begins to claim the poet's whole being, he senses its coming as a kind of "obscurity," the opposite of fame. The final appearance of the interior paramour argues an end to the unfulfilled desire which created the need for that paramour, and yet the absence of desire means a loss of selfhood as well. Of course, the poem itself remains poised on the verge of this disappearance, as Stevens lights "the first light of evening."

Since "Final Soliloquy of the Interior Paramour" is a poem about crossing over into the next "room," it raises many questions about whether or not Stevens envisions our passage as leading out of the mind, or into a deeper mental recess. What is the referent in "that which arranged the rendezvous, / Within its vital boundary, in the mind"? Vital, or living, boundary, might simply refer to the mind as a vital enclosure, a living space on *this* side. But might not the force which arranged the rendezvous be a force from the *other* side? Similarly, does "an order, a whole, a knowledge," refer to the "collect" Stevens has now become, or does it point to something beyond him? Since the triad of terms is governed by the phrase "We feel the obscurity of," it seems as if Stevens is sensing the imminence of dark, or obscured, truths. Now that the shroud has been sewn, the earthly work done, Stevens seems ready to build a dwelling for the mind:

> Out of this same light, out of the central mind,
> We make a dwelling in the evening air,
> In which being there together is enough.

This dwelling in the evening air, perhaps in the evening star itself, is a house built for and by the spirit. It is also a resting place, a tomb. It is never satisfied, the mind, never; but at the end of this poem, Stevens can at least say, "enough."

"Reality Is an Activity of the Most August Imagination" (1954) exemplifies the uncanny weightlessness of Stevens' last poems, with their "ease of mind that was like being alone in a boat at sea." Here Stevens is driving, a rare activity for that inveterate walker:

Last Friday, in the big light of last Friday night,
We drove home from Cornwall to Hartford, late.

It was not a night blown at a glassworks in Vienna
Or Venice, motionless, gathering time and dust.

There was a crush of strength in a grinding going round,
Under the front of the westward evening star,

The vigor of glory, a glittering in the veins,
As things emerged and moved and were dissolved,

Either in distance, change or nothingness,
The visible transformations of summer night,

An argentine abstraction approaching form
And suddenly denying itself away.

There was an insolid billowing of the solid.
Night's moonlight lake was neither water nor air.[13]

The opening sentence of the poem, describing a most ordinary evening activity, is nevertheless illuminated by the phrase "big light"; the master touch is revealed in the rejection of more ornate adjectives to describe the light and the glory that are still left. Stevens refuses to see the night as a completed, old-world artifact "gathering time and dust." With his own *Collected Poems* now on the shelf, the anxiety behind this deprecation is clear. As Stevens proves that he can see into the living strength of the night, he renews his own claim to poetic life. This renewal applies in two ways: first, it assures us that Stevens is still capable of sight and insight; second, it chastises the tendency to see a great poet's accomplishment as belonging to the past, to a "motionless" order. This is all familiar Stevensian doctrine. Where "Reality Is an Activity of the Most August Imagination" truly startles is in the ease with which it ascends to the sublime. For we move from a simple drive home to "a crush of strength in a grinding going round, / Under the front of the westward evening star." Suddenly the car has become a chariot, the great car not of the sun but of that evening star which so obsessed Stevens at the end. We blink at so outrageous and sudden a transformation, but it is unmistakable. Stevens leaves the chariot driverless, but we are free to imagine the poet himself holding the reins in "The vigor of glory, a glittering in the veins [reins?]." After all, "reality is an activity of the most august imagination," whose home must be the westward evening star, not Hartford. And the poet ascends of his own power, needing no elegist to place him among the constellations.

"The Poem That Took the Place of a Mountain" is Stevens' quiet answer to "Under Ben Bulben," which might be described as the mountain that took the place of a poem. Stevens chooses the mountain not so much for its solidity as for its view ("the outlook"):

There it was, word for word,
The poem that took the place of a mountain.

He breathed its oxygen,
Even when the book lay turned in the dust of his table.

It reminded him how he had needed
A place to go to in his own direction,

How he had recomposed the pines,
Shifted the rocks and picked his way among clouds,

For the outlook that would be right,
Where he would be complete in an unexplained
completion:

The exact rock where his inexactnesses
Would discover, at last, the view toward which they had
edged,

Where he could lie and, gazing down at the sea,
Recognize his unique and solitary home.

"There it was," rather than imply completion, compels us to imagine a temporal dimension in which such completion might occur, while at the same time "was" encourages our belief in such a possibility. "A place to go to in his own direction," followed by "picked his way among clouds," takes us all the way back to "The Death of a Soldier":

> When the wind stops and, over the heavens,
> The clouds go, nevertheless,
> In their direction.

Following after, Stevens too wanders lonely as a cloud. "Outlook" figures so importantly in this poem because Stevens is talking about seeing, not being, the truth of completion. Frenzy aside, this is that "old man's eagle mind" Yeats spoke of in "An Acre of Grass." From his aerie, "the exact rock," Stevens has attained the perspective toward which all his poems had "edged," in their "edgings and inchings of final form," to quote from the ending of "Ordinary Evening." Stevens' trope (if it can be called that) for his poems is "inexactnesses," an unbearably dry word, and yet a cunning one as well. As the longest word in the poem, and the one which takes the longest to utter, it forces the tongue to linger for a moment on what is to be left behind, as if Stevens were reluctant to abandon those "inexactnesses." Stevens contemplates a burial place ("where he could lie") which is both rock and outlook, solid ground and perspective, permanence and impermanence. In short, a home in the sea. No local place and habitation will hold Stevens, no Drumcliffe churchyard. As for the nature of the view itself, that is best described in the words of a recent critic writing on the end of Emerson's *Nature*:

> Yet in the end it is difficult to say whether the hope we are offered in "Prospects" belongs among the visions from Patmos or the views from Pisgah; whether we are being shown the Jerusalem in which we might someday live, or the Promised Land we will never be permitted to enter.[14]

"A Mythology Reflects Its Region" appears to be a poem about the truth of imagery in the obsolescence of a credible mythology. But the question of poetic accuracy, which did indeed obsess Stevens, amounts to only a side issue in the poem. For what Stevens terms "the image" is best thought of as a likeness—and the poem's true context, reinforced by its block-like appearance on the page, is epitaphic:

> A mythology reflects its region. Here
> In Connecticut, we never lived in a time
> When mythology was possible—But if we had—
> That raises the question of the image's truth.
> The image must be of the nature of its creator.
> It is the nature of its creator increased,
> Heightened. It is he, anew, in a freshened youth
> And it is he in the substance of his region,
> Wood of his forests and stone out of his fields
> Or from under his mountains.

"Substance of his region" should be read both as the place of burial and the materials out of which the tomb sculpture is fashioned. The poet himself meditates on the question of where and how to memorialize, or simply bury, the poet. As in "The River of Rivers in Connecticut," Stevens bequeaths himself to his land, girding with strength the region that strengthened him, just as the invisible river fertilized the source of fertility.

"Under his mountains" alerts us to the presence of "Under Ben Bulben," once again symbolizing the Yeatsian posture at death, from which Stevens will mark his divergence. He comes close to Yeats, however, in the emphasis on native soil; "stone out of his fields" answers to "limestone quarried near the spot." Stevens differs, however, in his avoidance of the spot of burial, as well as his refusal to mention an actual tomb. Stevens will not be bound in space, but chooses to be buried everywhere in the substance of his region: no institutions of burial can mediate his survival. Where there is no tomb there can be no visitors, so Stevens' epitaphic verse does not address a public audience.

A region lasts longer than a tomb, and for the space of this poem Stevens foregoes darker reflections on how even rocks and mountains can be pulverized. The poem's note of serenity, though, is difficult to gauge, since it may represent resignation as well as certainty over the poet's fate. I called "A Mythology Reflects Its Region" epitaphlike, but it reads more like a fragment of an epitaph, a part broken off from some larger structure, and in that fragmentary quality lies the paradox of its theme. Do we survive in more than fragmentary form even if we survive in the substance of our region? This anxiety is best expressed in "Two Illustrations That the World Is What You Make of It":

> He left half a shoulder and half a head
> To recognize him in after time.
>
> These marbles lay weathering in the grass
> When the summer was over, when the change
>
> Of summer and the sun, the life
> Of summer and the sun, were gone.

"Ariel was glad he had written his poems." It is hard to tell what is more surprising in this opening line of "The Planet on the Table": Stevens' name for himself, or his admission that poems are *written*, rather than chanted, intoned, or whatever. Complicating matters, of course, is the fact that this admission is made by "Ariel," a spirit standing for precisely that which cannot be written. Nowhere else in his poetry does Stevens bestow a name upon himself in this fashion; "Ariel" is neither his own invention, like "Hoon," nor ironic, like "Crispin." If we take the name to stand for airy essence, or spirit (sprite), Ariel may be a substitute for Psyche, the poet's breath embodied. Ariel is a playful spirit, and so Stevens puts on a deliberate casualness about the sources of his inspiration, ordering his canon under the simplest possible headings:

> Ariel was glad he had written his poems.
> They were of a remembered time
> Or of something seen that he liked.

Of particular interest in "The Planet on the Table" is the division Stevens creates between poem and maker, a distinction he is driven to make when he broods on the question of whether or not his poems will survive. Equating poetry with "makings of the sun," Stevens looks for analogues to survival in the fate of other natural things. What he finds can hardly offer much comfort:

> Other makings of the sun
> Were waste and welter
> And the ripe shrub writhed.

Nature, too, is mortal. "Welter" brings "Lycidas" to mind with its promise that the dead poet shall not be scattered and forgotten:

> He must not float upon his watery bier
> Unwept, and welter to the parching wind,
> Without the meed of some melodious tear.

But in "The Planet on the Table" the preservation of the poet and his works is very much at issue. Cast in the past tense, the poem has a hollow, elegiac sound, reinforced by alliterative play on the windy "*w*": were, waste, welter, was, which, words. If a great effort has not failed, then it is simply over. Looking back, Stevens appears to be saying farewell to the idea of literary survival, consoling himself with the craftsman's pride in having at least made it well:

> His self and the sun were one
> And his poems, although makings of his self,
> Were no less makings of the sun.
>
> It was not important that they survive.
> What mattered was that they should bear
> Some lineament or character,
>
> Some affluence, if only half-perceived,
> In the poverty of their words,
> Of the planet of which they were part.

A line such as "It was not important that they survive" masks the extent of Stevens' anxiety, which seems to encompass the fate of the whole "planet." After all, what is earth but another making of the sun? Ariel's written poems are part of the threatened planet, subject to its fate. Yet Ariel, of all characters, ought to be immune from the fate of matter. Like the sun, he is *apart from* the planet. (Might Stevens also be thinking of Uriel?) So Stevens equates Ariel's self and the sun, but not the self and its poems, which are called "makings of the sun." Stevens teases us with the possibility of identity between self, sun, and poems through the trickery of syntax—"His self and the sun were one / And his poems . . ."—but the sentence goes on to enforce the distinction. The intentional crudeness of "makings"—linked with "waste"—must be considered; poetry means "making," of course, but the plural lends a different cast to the word. "Makings of his self," taken alone, might induce one to believe that the self was composed of its creations, but in the context of the poem this does not make sense. Ariel's poems, on the contrary, were produced by a self that is now capable of detaching itself from its creations, expelling them, since that self is a poetic spirit, a source of energy in its own right. Ariel survives the breaking of the wand, the farewell to *materia poetica*.

The most extraordinary thing about "The Planet on the Table" is its combination of modesty and outrageousness: it was not important that they survive, since the self and sun are one. The poem's title, though it may refer to Stevens' *Collected Poems* (a world on the table), can probably be best explained by lines from "Someone Puts a Pineapple Together":

> It is as if there were three planets: the sun,
> The moon, and the imagination.[15]

In "The Planet on the Table," Stevens' self is with the sun and his poems with earth, storehouse of imagination, compendium of all we are. Stevens' anxieties stem from the vulnerability of that third planet. But even as he contemplates the possible destruction of what he has made, Stevens envisions some other version of survival, a mystical merging of self and sun. Perhaps that union has already occurred: for where is Stevens seeing from, that he can call the earth a planet on the table?

Written in the same year as "The Planet on the Table," "The River of Rivers in Connecticut" is an antithetical companion piece, returning to the planet of which it is part—albeit in a ghostly mode. Stevens insists on locating his anonymous river "far this side of Stygia," in the land of the living. At times, the river seems more like a glassy essence, or reflector:

> It is not to be seen beneath the appearances
> That tell of it. The steeple at Farmington
> Stands glistening and Haddam shines and sways.

In the words of "The Planet on the Table," the river bears "Some lineament or character" of its planet. But it seems to catch this planet at the point of irreality: glistening, shining, swaying. Indeed the river itself is "flashing and flashing," as if it were sending undecoded messages. Even though Stevens tells us that "the mere flowing of the water is a gayety," there is something more than a little disturbing about the unnamed river. For one thing, it seems to flow through a ghost town:

On its banks,

No shadow walks. The river is fateful,
Like the last one. But there is no ferryman.
He could not bend against its propelling force.

The thin men of Haddam have grown even thinner; the absence of shadows portends the absence of people. Are we on another urn? Perhaps more disturbing, or intriguing, is the fact that the river cannot be crossed. Crossing the Styx brings one to the underworld, a land of the dead, but also a land *after* death. What does it mean to remain *this* side of Stygia, where there is a steeple but no people? Presumably, it would mean remaining in life, except that this eerie uncharted river and its empty shimmering environs hardly seem filled with life. A more likely interpretation would take the river as a space between both lands, partaking of each in some measure but following its own course, leading neither to life nor death. Thus, the river is vital, yet somehow inimical to ordinary human life as well. The poem's last line bears out the final irreality of "the river that flows nowhere like a sea."

In "Repose of Rivers," Hart Crane actually speaks with the voice of a river as it charts its course to the sea. Stevens does not go this far, but we hardly need to be told that there is a deep affinity between the river of rivers and the course of his own poetic curriculum. Wordsworth called the Derwent, his native stream, "the fairest of all rivers"; Stevens' honorific for the Connecticut River of his spirit is even more hyperbolic. There may even be some trace of the Wordsworthian (and traditional) idea that rivers give birth to heroes. Certainly calling his river "like a sea" points to it as a pool of origins.

But I would read "The River of Rivers in Connecticut" more in terms of legacy than of origins, as Stevens' version of Whitman's bequeathal of himself to the land. Stevens' poems, his makings of the sun and river, become a felt presence in his native land. We could almost say that Stevens becomes a ghostly river here, a source of refreshment to his people. In "Directive," Frost leads his readers to "a brook that was the water of the house, / Cold as a spring as yet so near its source, / Too lofty and original to rage." Like "The River of Rivers in Connecticut," "Directive" ends with a command:

> Here are your waters and your watering-place.
> Drink and be whole again beyond confusion.

Stevens' imperative centers on the "curriculum" he leaves behind, for if curriculum reflects the pleasures of merely circulating, it also compels us to follow a course. The imperative to heed the river, if not to drink of its waters, is reinforced by Stevens' own command:

> Call it, once more, a river, an unnamed flowing,
>
> Space-filled, reflecting the seasons, the folk-lore
> Of each of the senses; call it, again and again,
> The river that flows nowhere, like a sea.

If "Call it" echoes the opening of *Moby-Dick*, then Ishmael's broodings on the lure of the sea are appropriate in Stevens' context. For Stevens wants his countrymen to call on him ("Call me . . ."), to turn his way. Yet he remains anonymous, an "unnamed flowing," for "The River of Rivers in Connecticut" will not admit that poems are written artifacts.

What can we say, then, about this poem as a meditation on survival, on poetic afterlife? When

Keats proposed "Here lies one whose name was writ in water" as his epitaph, he was lamenting evanescence, but Stevens chooses to sign his name in the river of rivers because it will continue to flow after his death. It may even outlast the planet of which it is part, since Stevens calls his unmapped river "the third commonness with light and air." However immaterial the river of rivers, it does preserve signs of familiarity, thus binding itself to some version of material survival, if only through imagery. The poet's fate as prophesied here is to remain part of the atmosphere of his region, an invisible current of water and air, for as long as that region lasts.

Stevens, who leaves us at least two of everything, also left two "death" poems, one of which ends the *Collected Poems*, the other *The Palm at the End of the Mind*. "Not Ideas about the Thing But the Thing Itself" has the prestige granted by the poet's designation, whereas the posthumous "Of Mere Being," whose opening line furnishes *Palm* with its title, probably has become the consensual favorite of readers. Indeed, "Of Mere Being" reads like an intentional revision of "Not Ideas," as if Stevens were aiming at making a new ending—or at least providing a more mysterious poem to occupy the final position.

> At the earliest ending of winter,
> In March, a scrawny cry from outside
> Seemed like a sound in his mind.

In the opening to "Not Ideas," Stevens may be remembering an earlier March poem, "The Sun This March," where the end of winter announced the return of a strong self accompanied by "voices as of lions." The poem begins in a naturalistic setting and then moves on to the vision of the colossal sun "Surrounded by its choral rings."

> That scrawny cry—It was
> A chorister whose c preceded the choir.
> It was part of the colossal sun,
>
> Surrounded by its choral rings,
> Still far away. It was like
> A new knowledge of reality.

"Cry" is metamorphosed into "choir"; the poem holds out the promise of a collectivity of singers. The glimpse of the beyond in "Not Ideas" is surprisingly orthodox for Stevens. Though he stands on the near side of death, so that the sun is "still far away," he sees the possibility of union. As in "The Planet on the Table," Stevens verges on equating self and sun. The scrawny cry of the bird, about to be absorbed by the sun's crescendo, heralds a judgment on the poet's own earthly sounds. And yet, in the interval before absorption, what remains fixed in the ear is the insistent, irreducible cry of the herald, however scrawny, prophesying and preventing its own disappearance.

"Of Mere Being" says nothing about the sun or choirs; it displays a fabricated world, though its "fire-fangled" bird may indeed come from the sun, the fire fashioner. The question toward which the poem leads is the Blakean one: who made thee, who formed thy symmetry? The "gold-feathered bird" stands gorgeously alone, as if the scrawny crier of "Not Ideas" were now transformed into something rich and strange, something *singular*—or self-begotten, if we read the bird as phoenix. If what the bird in "Not Ideas" augured was "like a new knowledge of reality," then this further cast of mind seems to be a *new* new knowledge, as Stevens verges ever closer to the "foreign meaning" of the other side.

> The palm at the end of the mind,
> Beyond the last thought, rises
> In the bronze decor,
>
> A gold-feathered bird
> Sings in the palm, without human meaning,
> Without human feeling, a foreign song.
>
> You know then that it is not the reason
> That makes us happy or unhappy.
> The bird sings. Its feathers shine.
>
> The palm stands on the edge of space.
> The wind moves slowly in the branches.
> The bird's fire-fangled feathers dangle down.

The palm at the end of the mind, a destination and a reward, symbolizes both resurrection and poetic glory: as the palm rises, so do we. Like the soldier, in "Metaphors of a Magnifico," Stevens sees a tree in the distance, though there is no assurance that the "edge of space" beckons on to a village, much less the walled city of Jerusalem. Much rides on whether or not "the end of the mind" and "Beyond the last thought" are synonymous, or whether Stevens implies that there is a space *between* the last thought and mind's end, a region that lies within the mind but beyond the range of thought. "It is not the reason / That makes us happy or unhappy" might point to this region. If one chooses to equate the two phrases, then the palm would rise, the bird's feathers "dangle down," just beyond the mind's edge: "It would have been outside," to quote from "Not Ideas." Wherever we stand in space, "bronze decor," with its echoes of

Horace's claim for poetry—*exegi monumentum aere perennior*—and the string of words in the final line, convince us that bird and palm alike blaze with artifice. Yet the maker or fashioner remains unidentified. "Of Mere Being" is poised on the edge of unanswerable questions. Does the wind move slowly because it is dying down, as the spirit departs in death? Or does it move slowly because a new life is starting up? Whose spirit is this?

As I end this chapter and this book, I want to stay within the spirit of these forms of farewell. So many of Stevens' last poems are concerned with the poet's uncanny legacy that it seems appropriate to close with a living emblem of his continued presence in the work of a later poet. The natural place to go would be the poetry of John Ashbery. Stevens' legacy to Ashbery, insofar as it can be rationally discriminated, takes several forms. First, the Ashbery who has always paid homage to the occlusions of random facts, who has always been beguiled by surface appearances, speaks for the Stevens of *Parts of a World.* But then there is the Ashbery who proves increasingly apocalyptic, concerned with vision and revelation; this version of the poet seems to be obsessed with "The Auroras of Autumn." There is a passage in "Fragment," Ashbery's first truly successful long poem, where the presence of Stevens is made startlingly clear.

> Out of this intolerant swarm of freedom as it
> Is called in your press, the future, an open
> Structure, is rising even now, to be invaded by the
>   present
> As the past stands to one side, dark and theoretical

Yet most important of all, for his midnight
  interpretation
Is suddenly clasped to you with the force of a hand
But a clear moonlight night in which distant
Masses are traced with parental concern.
After silent, colored storms the reply quickly
Wakens, has already begun its life, its past, just whole
  and sunny.

Thus reasoned the ancestor, and everything
Happened as he had foretold, but in a funny kind of way.

A few stanzas earlier, Ashbery had announced himself ready "To persist in the revision of very old / Studies, as though mounted on a charger," and the chivalric or quest metaphor continues in this passage. As usual with Ashbery, there is an uncanny alternation of abstract and concrete tropes: where we would expect to find a castle, instead we glimpse an "open structure." When we read "As the past stands to one side, dark and theoretical," I think we are meant to fill in the Lady of Romance. Yet the lady turns out to be no lady at all, but a parent, an ancestor, as the next stanza will go on to inform us. So his companion, no longer an erotic ideal, has become something of a magus, a friendly wizard offering his midnight interpretation. The turn in "Fragment" from the beloved toward the poem's true subject could not be clearer. Ashbery quests for a kind of visionary wisdom or gnosis, rather than for erotic comfort. And it should not be too difficult to identify this Merlin persona. "Silent, colored storms": these must be the auroras, and whose key signature are they, if not Stevens'? So the poet survives, not only as a sign in the sky, but as a near presence clasped to us "with the force of a hand."

Notes
Index

Notes

Preface

1. Helen Vendler, *On Extended Wings: Wallace Stevens' Longer Poems* (Cambridge, Mass.: Harvard University Press, 1969).

2. Harold Bloom, *Wallace Stevens: The Poems of Our Climate* (Ithaca, N.Y.: Cornell University Press, 1977).

3. Frank Kermode, *The Sense of an Ending* (New York: Oxford University Press, 1967).

4. Lawrence Lipking, *The Life of the Poet: Beginning and Ending Poetic Careers* (Chicago: University of Chicago Press, 1981).

5. Richard Poirier, "Writing Off the Self," *Raritan* 1 (1981): 106–133.

6. Ibid., p. 125.

Chapter 1

1. All citations of Stevens' poetry are to *The Collected Poems of Wallace Stevens* (New York: Alfred A. Knopf, 1954), except where otherwise noted.

2. The exact quotation reads: "Why should we fear to be crushed by savage elements, we who are made up of the same elements?"

3. Vendler, *On Extended Wings*, p. 207.

4. "The Course of a Particular," is to be found in Wallace Stevens, *Opus Posthumous*, ed. Samuel French Morse (New York: Alfred A. Knopf, 1959).

5. *Letters of Wallace Stevens*, ed. Holly Stevens (New York: Alfred A. Knopf, 1967), p. 469.

6. Bloom, *The Poems of Our Climate*, p. 231.

7. Ibid., p. 234.

8. Poirier, "Writing Off the Self," p. 126.

9. Richard Ellmann, *Eminent Domain* (New York: Oxford University Press, 1967), p. 120.

10. Wallace Stevens, *The Necessary Angel: Essays on Reality and the Imagination* (New York: Random House, 1951), p. 26.

11. Helen Vendler, *Part of Nature, Part of Us* (Cambridge, Mass.: Harvard University Press, 1980), p. 26.

Chapter 2

1. Vendler, *On Extended Wings*, p. 246.

2. Ibid., p. 231.

3. Holly Stevens, *Souvenirs and Prophecies* (New York: Alfred A. Knopf, 1977), pp. 253–254.

4. Ibid., p. 255.

5. The quotation appears in the epigraph to James Merrill's *Mirabell: Books of Number* (New York: Atheneum, 1968).

6. Vendler, *On Extended Wings*, p. 247.

7. See Frost's poem "Fire and Ice."

8. Vendler, *On Extended Wings*, p. 258.

9. Ibid.

10. Bloom, *The Poems of Our Climate*, pp. 266–267.

11. John Keats, "Sleep and Poetry," line 237.

12. Stevens, *Letters*, p. 636.

13. "The Noble Rider and the Sound of Words" is to be found in Stevens, *The Necessary Angel*.

14. Bloom, *The Poems of Our Climate*, p. 275.

15. William Wordsworth, *The Prelude*, Book 1, lines 269 ff.

16. Bloom, *The Poems of Our Climate*, p. 306.

17. The word appears in John Ashbery's "Syringa," from *Houseboat Days* (New York: Viking Press, 1977).

18. Susan Sontag, "Writing Itself: On Roland Barthes," *New Yorker*, April 26, 1982, p. 124.

Chapter 3

1. Vendler, *On Extended Wings*, p. 236.
2. Stevens, *Letters*, p. 636–637.
3. Vendler also notes the link to Yeats; see *On Extended Wings*, p. 280.
4. The quotation can be found in Milton's "Of Education."
5. See Keats's sonnet "Bright Star."
6. J. Hillis Miller, *Poets of Reality: Six Twentieth-Century Writers* (Cambridge, Mass.: Harvard University Press, 1966), p. 274.
7. "A Discovery of Thought" is to be found in Stevens, *Opus Posthumous*.
8. Vendler, *On Extended Wings*, p. 296.

Chapter 4

1. Peter Sacks, "The Divine Translation: Elegiac Aspects of *The Changing Light at Sandover*," in David Lehman and Charles Berger, eds., *James Merrill: Essays in Criticism* (Ithaca, N.Y.: Cornell University Press, 1983), p. 160.
2. Bloom, *The Poems of Our Climate*, p. 292.
3. Stevens, *Letters*, p. 358.
4. Bloom, *The Poems of Our Climate*, pp. 283–284.
5. Ibid., p. 281.
6. Stevens, *Letters*, p. 552.
7. See the chapter entitled "Time and the Keeping of Poetry," in Richard Poirier, *Robert Frost: The Work of Knowing* (New York: Oxford University Press, 1977).
8. Bloom, *The Poems of Our Climate*, p. 285.
9. The phrase comes from an alternative title to the section of "Owl's Clover" entitled "Mr. Burnshaw and the Statue." See Stevens, *Letters*, p. 289.
10. "Of Mere Being" is to be found in Stevens, *Opus Posthumous*.
11. Wordsworth, 1850 *Prelude*, line 45.
12. "A Mythology Reflects Its Religion" is to be found in Stevens, *Opus Posthumous*.
13. Stevens, *Letters*, p. 761.
14. For a contrasting vision of church bells, see "The Old Lutheran Bells at Home."

Chapter 5

1. Stevens, *Letters*, pp. 617–618.

2. Lipking, *The Life of the Poet*, p. 138.

3. Ibid., p. 169.

4. Ibid., p. 172.

5. Ibid.

6. "A Child Asleep in Its Own Life," *Opus Posthumous*, p. 106.

7. Frank Kermode, "Dwelling Poetically in Connecticut," in Frank Doggett and Robert Buttel, eds. *Wallace Stevens: A Celebration* (Princeton: Princeton University Press, 1980), p. 264.

8. Edward Said, *Beginnings* (New York: Basic Books, 1975), p. 229.

9. Ibid., p. 227.

10. See the lectures "Effects of Analogy" in Stevens, *The Necessary Angel*.

11. Frost uses the phrase in letters of July 4, 1913, and February 22, 1914, both to John T. Bartlett. See Elaine Barry, *Robert Frost on Writing* (New Brunswick, N.J.: Rutgers University Press, 1973), pp. 59, 63.

12. Keats to John Taylor, February 27, 1818.

13. "Reality Is an Activity of the Most August Imagination" is to be found in Stevens, *Opus Posthumous*.

14. B. L. Packer, *Emerson's Fall* (New York: Continuum, 1982), p. 84.

15. "Someone Puts a Pineapple Together" is to be found in Stevens, *Opus Posthumous*.

Index